Loretta J

MOUNTAIN HOMESPUN

MOUNTAIN HOMESPUN

BY

FRANCES LOUISA GOODRICH

A facsimile of the original,
published in 1931,
with a new introduction
by Jan Davidson

The University of Tennessee Press
KNOXVILLE

Publication of this book has been assisted by a grant
from the Southern Highland Handicraft Guild.

The paper in this book meets the minimum requirements
of the American National Standard for Permanence of Paper
for Printed Library Materials.
∞
The binding materials have been chosen for strength and durability.

Library of Congress Cataloging in Publication Data

Goodrich, Frances Louisa.
  Mountain homespun : a facsimile of the original, published in 1931 /
  Frances Louisa Goodrich : with a new introduction by Jan Davidson.
    p. cm.
  Bibliography: p.
  Includes index.
  ISBN 0–87049–620–4 (cloth: alk. paper)
    1. Hand weaving–North Carolina. 2. Handicraft–North Carolina.
  3. Mountain whites (Southern States)–North Carolina. I. Title.
TT848.G665 1989   89–33843
746.1′4′097568–dc20   CIP

CONTENTS

ILLUSTRATIONS

ACKNOWLEDGMENTS

Thanks first to Eleanor B. Goodrich and Mary Hilliker, who shared Aunt Fan with me.

Thanks to the people at the Jackson County Public Library, Sylva, NC; Holderness, NH, Public Library; WCU Special Collections, Hunter Library, Cullowhee, NC; Pack Memorial Library, Asheville, NC; Berea College Library and Appalachian Center, Berea, KY; Presbyterian Historical Society, Philadelphia, PA; Western Reserve Historical Society, Cleveland, OH.; Yale University School of Fine Arts Library and Yale University Press, New Haven, CT.; Mars Hill College Library and Rural Life Museum, Mars Hill, NC; Madison County Public Library, Marshall, NC; Western Office of the North Carolina Division of Archives and History, Asheville, NC; Smithsonian Institution Traveling Exhibition Service, Washington, DC; Southern Highland Collection, University of North Carolina at Asheville; Southern Highland Handicraft Guild, Asheville, NC; Southern Historical Collection and North Carolina Collection, University of North Carolina, Chapel Hill, NC; and Office of the Curator, The White House, Washington, DC.

Thanks to Grover Angel, Barry Bergey, Richard Blaustein, Chris Bobbitt, Lewis Buck, Delos Cook, Mary Delashmitt, Richard Dillingham, George Frizzell, Jim Gentry, Alice Hardin, Bess Hawes, the Reverend William Herd, George Holt, Laurel Horton, Germaine Juneau, Doris Kennedy, Loyal Jones, Susan Leveille, Gordon McKinney, Bonell and Jerry McMillan, Eric Olson, Dan Patterson, Frank B. Shelton, David Whisnant, Blair White, Max Williams, and Sadye Tune Wilson.

Thanks to the people at the Mountain Heritage Center, Western Carolina University: Tyler Blethen, David Brewin, Diane Collins, Joan Greene, Michael Kline, Pat Montee, Barbara Reimensnyder, Gloria Sandborg, and Curtis Wood; and to those upstairs—James Dooley, Myron Coulter, and C. D. Spangler.

Thanks to all the Western North Carolina families who loaned family treasures for *Coverlets: New Threads in Old Patterns* in both its Mountain Heritage Center and Smithsonian (SITES) versions.

To the Davidsons—John, Kathleen, Kay, John Neil, and Chloe—thanks for being mountain people. Most thanks must go to two weaving women: Suzanne McDowell, who pointed out the trail, and Nanette Davidson, who made it possible for me to travel it.

INTRODUCTION

Seams Like Old Times

In the course of researching an exhibit project called *Coverlets: New Threads in Old Patterns,* to be sponsored by the National Endowment for the Arts Folklife program, the Mountain Heritage Center staff borrowed about 40 old coverlets made between 1850 and 1930 in ten Western North Carolina counties. We began to notice that the coverlets, all made by piecing narrow strips together, had two kinds of seams: matched and unmatched. As the stories of the coverlets unfolded, it appeared that those with matched seams (in which the motifs meet precisely across the seam, giving the illusion of one piece of cloth) were generally made after 1900 and that most of those known to have been made earlier were of the crooked-seam variety. The straight-seam ones turned out to be, not surprisingly, the work of professional or semi-professional weavers, many of whom had some connection to the Penland School of Crafts at Penland, the John C. Campbell Folk School at Brasstown, or the Southern Highland Handicraft Guild, headquartered in Asheville, all North Carolina institutions that grew out of the era of northern Protestant ameliorative work in Appalachia from the 1870s to the 1920s. Many of the local weavers also had some family tradition of weaving, which had been stimulated by the markets and refined by the craft teaching established by the "fotched-on" [Appalachian for "brought in"] women—the missionaries from the north. One of the standards insisted upon by the northern ladies was that the seams of a coverlet be straight.

The most fascinating coverlet was the brown Double Bowknot now owned by the Southern Highland Handicraft Guild, which is labeled "This is the coverlet that started the Allanstand Industries." Before it was a museum piece, it was used by Frances Goodrich to personify the continuity of her handicraft revival; to raise funds for craft programs, schools and hospitals; to star in the most dramatic moment of Goodrich's *Mountain Homespun;* and to launch a business that, in a fashion, survives to this writing, five years short of a century old. Before Goodrich got it about 1895, it was a bedspread, probably greatly loved by an old mountain family because one of them made it completely herself. It is a crooked-seam coverlet made about 1850.

In Wilson and Kennedy's *Of Coverlets* and in old photographs like the one of that wonderful Leatherwood family with straw hats, we began to notice that a coverlet was hung as a backdrop by many of the families for the important occasion of being photographed – almost as if it represented members of the family long gone. The families we talked to who had kept coverlets into the 1980s had no doubt that they symbolized the family in some ways. Besides the connections to the weaver of the past, there is something else familial about the old coverlets – perhaps their warmth and connection to the marriage bed. Coverlets were a common wedding gift, a favorite present to make for each of one's sons and daughters, and a special item in the long list of kinds of cloth made on mountain farmsteads. One old coverlet had been the first thing, after the people, to be rescued from a burning house.

Before the handicraft revival of the 1890s, there were community weavers who took in spun wool and made it into coverlets, and there were also many families in which woven goods were neither bought nor sold, but produced solely for the family's use. Overshot pattern weaving in the "double drafts," a demanding kind of weaving, was probably done infrequently by family weavers, who were more often engaged in making plainer fabrics for clothing and other uses.

To produce a straight-seam coverlet, the loom must be tight and accurate and the weaver must "beat" every shot of the weft with equal force. When the beat is weaker, the motifs are longer; when stronger, they are compacted. Someone who does not practice at the overshot weaving will likely be unable to make a matched-seam coverlet. Another reason offered for the crooked seams was that the old way of washing coverlets, in the cold water of the stream was easier if the seams were taken apart. Sometimes the strips were sewn back together in a different order so as to distribute the wear evenly. Still another technical answer for crooked seams resides in the nature of the loom. The old "barn" or "porch" looms were big, loose affairs on which it was difficult even for a skilled weaver to keep an even beat on the cloth; accordingly, motifs became squashed or elongated by uneven beating. When strips of such cloth are placed side by side, the motifs will not match and the seams will appeared crooked. The missionary ladies procured small, efficient looms for their weavers that made keeping an even beat easier.

The seams of a coverlet are probably not very important in the great scheme of things and the explanatory power of objects is severely limited, but a comparison of a Penland coverlet from the 1920s with a family-made coverlet from the 1880s reveals obvious differences, which resulted from the organization and professionalization of crafts by missionaries. In observing what the missionary cultural programs wrought, it is important to try to understand what they displaced. Several mountain ladies told us that the older coverlets had "honest seams" and several others that " a crooked seam throws the devil off your track." The difference between a crooked seam and a straight one may be a matter of concept. To a woman who dismantled the coverlet into strips to wash it and then sewed them back in whichever order would distribute the wear, the thing was a set of pieces. To Goodrich, perhaps, it was a bedspread, which ought to appear as much like whole cloth as possible. But the missionaries, having no doubts about the superiority of their own culture, assumed that their artistic judgments and ideas of "quality" were the only correct ones. As in many other points of encounter between Appalachia and the dominant culture, the labor and resources were Appalachian, while the decisions made and the ideas behind them were "fotched-on."

Today, an innovative, eclectic, personal tradition of skills—mostly held by native mountain elders—lives next door to a professionalized, quality-conscious, object-oriented, market-wise craft business. Each is, in its own way, "Appalachian handicrafts." Each has a long and interesting history, the one finding its roots in necessity, the other in a "systematic cultural intervention."[1] The revival tradition, with intellectual and social as well as economic ramifications, finds its roots in the Social Gospel and its spiritual grandfathers among the likes of John Ruskin, William Morrris, and Gustav Stickley.[2] The older tradition's practitioners find their spiritual grandparents among their actual grandfathers and grandmothers.

Was there any harm done in Frances Goodrich's telling her weavers to make the seams straight? Or to make table runners, pillow covers, dresser scarves, or overshot with cotton wefts? Those who could not weave up to a standard set by Goodrich were told to try spinning, or carding, or she would try to find other work for them in the Industries. Inevitably, in going from farm families to farm-and-craft families, people gave up some of their independence to organizers like Goodrich. Compared to the factory whistle, however, Goodrich's occasional prodding and quality control left those who worked for her with considerable control over their time, if not their designs. By 1900, the alternative was present, as textile mill recruiters worked among rural mountaineers, trying to get them to move to mill towns, where even the children would be employed.[3] In Madison County, North Carolina, industrialization appeared in the form of the Capitola Manufacturing Company (1903) in Marshall.[4] Craft work, Goodrich believed, was a way for the people to stay on their family farms until the blessings of education and community would allow them to build Appalachia into New England, or at least a reasonable facsimile.

Goodrich had other reasons for wanting straight seams, most notably the influence of museum-quality coverlets that had been on display in New England in "Colonial" period rooms. Some old New Englanders (probably professionals in the more densely populated centers where crafts that were domestic chores elsewhere had become trades) had made straight-seam coverlets, and their descendents in the market centers like New York, Chicago, Cleveland, and Boston would want straight seams for their Colonial Revival bedrooms. Part of Frances Goodrich's makeup was a refined sense of neatness. The essence of the Colonial Revival vision, Celia Betsky has pointed out, is what Emily Dickinson called "to see New Englandy." Goodrich had that kind of vision, and her success or failure in the mountains depended on how well, at each of its many points of encounter with mountain people, that vision accommodated the realities of Appalachia.

One sortie in the neatness campaign probably came about when Frances Goodrich sat down to write to the mission board and had to force herself to write her letter's place of origin as "Sodom." According to local tradition, Sodom residents gloried in the humor of sharing the name of the town so evil that it was destroyed by the Lord.[5] Frances Goodrich saw no humor in it:

We felt that the name of Sodom was demoralizing and so on my second visit I had a chance to tell the people so. . . . To my surprise there were a large number of men in the house, and finding that a meeting of citizens was being held to decide about building a "church-house"– I made bold to enter, and ask how they felt about my coming to give them a school. Some are terribly afraid of our supposed heresies and I wanted them to have a chance to see one of "them women." . . . After they all had spoken, I opened fire on the name of the place. There was, of course, danger of stirring them up the wrong way and making them sulky and dogged about it, but frank speech is the safest and some consciences were reached as was evident afterwards. I told them such a name caused them all to think lightly of sin and that their children would be ashamed bye and bye to tell where they had come from. Jackson Ramsay was hard hit and another man told me that they didn't want people to think they "thought as lightly of the Almighty" as the name would show. I hope they will change the post office, but it is too soon to tell.[6]

In 1903, the name of the Sodom Post Office was changed to the suitably New Englandy name "Revere."

Like Sodom, the weaving tradition was a part of mountain life that needed to be tidied up and straightened out. Goodrich and others wrote often of "preserving" the old ways, but they changed the aesthetics, the production systems, the motivation for producing, the methods of teaching and learning, the materials, the designs, the tools, the ultimate destination of the products, the location where the work was done, and, eventually, who was doing it. They preserved some of the techniques and found ways to make objects that evoked the past but were very much made in the present. The irony of the old brown Double Bowknot that started Allanstand – the grand icon of the Appalachian handicraft revival – is that it could not have been sold as an Allanstand coverlet, because, like most old mountain coverlets, it has crooked seams and a mistake in the weaving.

At this writing, The Double Bowknot is touring the country on a Smithsonian-sponsored tour of museums, the log cabin where Goodrich sold crafts is a real estate office, the Southern Highland Handicraft Guild (in many ways, a Goodrich creation) is a powerful arbiter of craft work in a profession that supports or supplements the income of thousands of families, and Sodom is still called Sodom.

Changes Loom

At the center of *Mountain Homespun* is a coverlet or, more accurately, the gift of a coverlet from an Appalachian woman to a Yankee missionary – a "fotched-on woman" – who had come to uplift the mountain people. Since Frances Louisa Goodrich will forever be grouped with the fotched-on women, it is fair to try to answer where she was fotched from, how and to where, and for what purpose. As David Whisnant put it,

Where did they come from – geographically, economically, intellectually, politically, culturally? What sort of institutions and programs did they put together? How did local people react to them? What images of the mountains, mountain people, and fotched-on work did they project to a larger public, and with what effect? And what happened in the mountains as a result of their efforts?[7]

Some of what the missionaries did in the mountains, the hospitals, the schools, the fairs, and the craft business was greatly appreciated by the mountaineers, while some of the propaganda that was written to support the mission work was not. "They said we were all dumb bunnies," said one otherwise grateful Madison Countian. In the memories of those who knew her, Frances Goodrich was seen as a friend and ally of the mountain people.[8] Jacqueline Painter, who wrote an approving history of a mission school in Madison County, nonetheless speaks for many other mountaineers in saying,

While fully appreciating the benefits of the Presbyterians, I still bristle somewhat at the Northerners' condescensions, and resent the fact that often portrayed to the outside world were some of the worst examples of mountain poverty and ignorance.[9]

Craft work was, and is, criticized as romantic and uneconomical, perhaps nowhere more vehemently than in Thomas Dawley's *The Child that Toileth Not.*

Dawley tells of a 1907 encounter with a craftsperson in Madison County. Like most mountaineers in Dawley's book, the family lives in immoral squalor. When Dawley gives a little boy a nickel and asks what he will buy with it, the boy says "Meat" instead of candy and Dawley reacts,

> Now mark you! This was the home of a basket-maker! Basket making is the industry taught in our mountain mission schools by good, self-sacrificing women and men, who condemn the cotton mill.[10]

Dawley, of course, had the answer to the "mountain problem"—turn the whole region into a national park, and relocate the people in cotton mill work. Dawley was the classic case of an outsider who came to the mountains looking for trouble, and found it. Everything he found pointed toward the cotton mill: from idle, violent, unambitious men and "slattern-looking" women to squalid homes and inadequate diet.

Frances Goodrich came to the mountains looking for good to do, and without stretching the case, she found much of it to be done. She came, as many of the fotched-on women did, from old New England families with a heritage of public service. Goodrich's background of scholars, politicians, and divines was probably not unusual nor was her interest in social service to be unexpected, but her training was not, like that of colleagues, at Vassar, Wellesley, or Smith, but at art school. She was one of the first to envision the uplift of the mountain people through crafts and to create a market for mountain products. What did she preserve? What did she change?

One method of craft production that had survived in Western North Carolina was home-centered and conducted completely on a single farmstead, like that of Squire Daniel Wesley Angel (1838–1897) on the Paint Fork of Ivy. His wife, Lucy Catherine Ray Angel, and unmarried daughters, Nancy Jane (1861–1924) and Clarissa Cordelia (1866–1925), helped shear the sheep, dye the wool, wash it, card it, spin it, warp the loom, and weave coverlets.[11] When Goodrich first started the craft program at Brittain's Cove and got her first batch of wool ready, it was to the Angels that she took it to be woven. In three weeks, she received three finished coverlets, which were sold up north. Goodrich continued to "put out" weaving to the Angels and others, and to arrange classes in which master weavers like Elmeda Walker taught young women like Louise Payne the finer points of weaving. The Angels probably continued to weave for local people at lower rates than Goodrich paid. Goodrich clearly admired the Angels, but she did not choose to emulate the one-family method of production. She standardized the designs, chose which patterns were to be woven, supervised colors, and rejected work that was not up to her standards. She insisted on straight, matching seams in the coverlet, which meant that the weaver had to keep a consistently even beat through all the long yards of fabric. The weaver needed an accurate, well-balanced loom to produce work of that level of precision. By the early 1910s, Goodrich was supplying North Carolina weavers with Scandinavian-type looms of the kind introduced by Anna Ernberg, the Swedish-born director of Berea (Kentucky) College's weaving program.

Rather than preserving the old ways of production, Goodrich introduced a system of production that tied the workers to her. She not only provided the tools, the market, and the money, but she made the decisions. One reason for "putting out" the work—assigning some workers to card, some to spin, some to weave, and paying them by the pound, skein, or yard—was that more people could be employed. Some who could not weave could spin, some who could not spin could card, and the benefits of the program were thus available to more people, more families would be touched by "healthful interest," and more people would share in the money from sales. It could be argued that by paying for piecework, Goodrich was leaving in the workers' hands the decisions about how much to produce, and how soon. Goodrich always saw crafts as a supplement to farm work and, rightly done, a pleasure to the maker that could be indulged in at "dodge times." In this, and in most of her activities, Goodrich was more appreciative of the rhythms and styles of mountaineer life than many of her missionary contemporaries. Where others saw only idleness and self-fotched poverty, Goodrich, while accepting the basic shared attitude of the missionaries (mountaineers were poor because they were "thriftless," but like children they could be taught values) was better able than most to see beyond groupings of class and region and judge people as individuals. In the old mountain women, she found thrift, hard work, wisdom, insight, and lore that she thought should be passed on to the younger mountain women.

Goodrich aimed most of all to give the women a place to go and get together and do business of their own that mattered in the real world. It takes nothing away from her achievements to note that she maintained so much decision-making power in her own person at least partly to keep the women all personally involved with her. An important methodology of settlement work was the teaching of the subtleties of civilization through example. The more time a mountain woman spent with Miss Goodrich, the more she would be able to benefit from having the proper life exemplified on her behalf. Through the craft business, Goodrich always had a good reason to visit and keep up with the happenings in various families.

Much of Goodrich's was "women's work," but she was never reticent to challenge the male power structure. Her attitude toward the Laurel Country was maternal and protective. She was acutely aware of the changes taking place in mountain life:

> To us who have cast in our lot with the dwellers in the mountains to live and die with them, the problem of their future is now full of interest. Swift changes are taking place. On every side new forces push in.[12]

Contemporaneous with Goodrich's arrival in Madison County, the logging business began in earnest, bringing great social and environmental changes to the mountains. The timber boom took its local form as a splash dam on the Laurel River that periodically released a large volume of water to propel logs downstream. Goodrich felt that these fluxions were endangering those along the stream and was certain that the loss of bridges and footlogs (destroyed by the mass of cut logs) was preventing some mothers from attending mothers' meetings and from sending their children to school. She sought out Mr. Morrow of the Putnam Lumber Company and "had much conversation on lumbering and splash dams."[13]

When a plan was released in 1900 that would have included the Laurel Country in a proposed national park,[14] Goodrich rushed to Asheville to seek out Dr. Chase P. Ambler, the head of the pro-park movement and

> was satisfied from what he told me that the risk of our being included when the scheme was carried out is very slight indeed. The whole thing is remote and visionary as yet but I wish to take no chances. I went also to see Mr. Richards of the Southern RR who is such a fine friend of our schools, and an influential man.
>
> The reasons for the Laurel Country being left out of the park are these:
>
> First. The scheme as mapped out is too large. They are asking for a great deal more than they expect to get.
>
> Second. We are so near the railroad that the land will be too high even if condemned to purchase for such a purpose.
>
> Third. There is no heavy timber here, and the best that is left will be taken out in another year or two; whereas the promoters of the movement don't expect to have anything done for a number of years, much as they are pushing the matter.
>
> Fourth. It would be impracticable to close up in a measure as a park with its regulations would do the thoroughfare between the two states. Allanstand is in the most convenient road through since the mountains are not so high there as they are to the East and West.
>
> Dr. Ambler, the secretary of the association admitted that what they had laid out could not possibly be done, and that he had no idea of its being done to its full extent.[15]

Her reasoned attack on the park was typical of her well-planned, passionately-directed projects. The five-foot-one-inch-tall Miss Goodrich studied maps of the mountains and projected her campaign in the Shelton Laurel like a Presbyterian Napoleon.

Whence Fotched?

Frances Louisa Goodrich was born September 5, 1856, in Binghamton, New York, the third daughter of a Presbyterian minister, William Henry Goodrich of New Haven, and his wife, Mary Prichard Goodrich of Boston. Mary could count among her ancestors no fewer than seven Mayflower passengers, while William had only one, Governor Bradford. William had for his maternal grandfather Noah Webster, author of the *Dictionary* and of the most widely-used textbook of the day, the "Blueback Speller." William Goodrich's father was the Reverend Chauncey Allen Goodrich, Yale professor of rhetoric, son of Elizur Goodrich, Yale professor of law, son of the Reverend Elizur Goodrich, Yale professor of mathematics and astronomy.[16] After receiving his doctorate of divinity, William chose not to follow his ancestors' academic footsteps to New Haven, instead accepting a pastorate in Binghamton. The young minister and his family were part of a larger westward migration of New Englanders who followed the canals and railroads to the new, bustling cities of New York State and Ohio. To places like Binghamton went New England tradesmen, farmers, and entrepreneurs, and the custodians of New England culture, like William Goodrich.

In the summer of 1858, William Goodrich was called to be assistant pastor of the First Presbyterian Church, known as "The Old Stone Church," in Cleveland, Ohio, the booming former capital of Connecticut's Western Reserve. Little Frances (called Fanny) and her older sisters Julia and Mary stayed in Binghamton until a house was found in Cleveland. They arrived by train on Fanny's second birthday at a house on Superior Street between Bond and Wood. According to Julia, who was Frances' lifelong companion, their childhood was an exciting time.[17] They were in many ways at the center of Cleveland's social, religious, and political life. William was an abolitionist Republican who preached against slavery as "the great iniquity." Julia recalled,

There was so much excitement at the time of Lincoln's election and when Fort Sumter was fired upon, that the youngest of us could not but have these events stamped on her memory. Lincoln stopped in Cleveland on his way to his first inauguration and Father was one of the reception committee.[18]

The little girls met Lincoln and heard him speak. William planned to enlist as a Union army chaplain, but when the church's senior pastor, Dr. Samuel Aiken, died soon after the war began, William was elevated to the main pastorate and gave up his plans for a chaplaincy as he felt he was more needed in the church. He visited the nearby Camp Cleveland regularly and was named honorary chaplain of the Cleveland Grays.

Among William's homefront duties was helping to arrange for Cleveland's "Sanitary Fair," a ten-day event to raise funds for the Red Cross–like U.S. Sanitary Commission's work at the battlefields. One day at the fair, Julia and Frances admired a small, working scale model of a woodburning iron cookstove and the manufacturer gave it to their father, who set it up for the girls in the woodshed. In a pattern that would be repeated countless times in their subsequent forty-six years of housekeeping together, Frances chopped the wood and Julia cooked. The girls virtually moved to the woodshed, where they read books and prepared complete meals of greens, fried potatoes, biscuits (cut out with a thimble), and fried apples—all cooked in tiny cast-iron pans. The girls' best friends were the two daughters of railroad tycoon Amasa Stone: Clara, who later was wed to Secretary of State John Hay, and Flora, who became the wife of copper millionaire Samuel Mather. "The playhouse," Julia wrote, "had a good roof (to which the nimblest child, F.L.G., could climb), two windows and a door. We played keeping store in it and made real bonnets out of colored paper for sale."

William Goodrich's activities remained completely on the home front until the spring of 1865, when he saw war firsthand. Under the auspices of the U.S. Sanitary Commission, William was sent to Virginia to be with the army. He conducted services in hospital tents, wrote letters for dying men, and dressed the wounds of those who were brought in from the battlefield nearby. After only ten days, Goodrich became so ill that he had to leave. He worsened during the long trip back to Ohio and was "hardly able to get home." The encounter left him physically and emotionally scarred, and he was never the same again.

The war, Julia wrote, "was very real to us."

The Goodrich girls encountered Abraham Lincoln again, as his funeral procession passed their house and an unbroken line of mourners went by for a rainy day and night to view the President's remains.

In 1866, the family moved uptown, to a house on Euclid Avenue between Case and Stirling Avenues. The old plank road still ran on the north side of Euclid, and "covered wagons of emigrants passed" the Goodrich home on their way West. The girls took the streetcars to Cleveland Academy and other private schools.

"The Old Stone Church" was the focus of their childhood. "We children," Julia wrote, "thought that Father owned it and were grieved when we learned that it did not belong to him. We loved to visit him in his study, when he was not too busy to have us there. Sometimes Mother sent us with messages to him. We liked to slip into the empty church and climb into the pulpit to see how it would seem to be a preacher." When Frances was fourteen, she and Julia started teaching Sunday school.

Even aside from the war's effects, comfortable Protestant churches were changing in the mid-1800s, especially in the growing urban areas. Some wealthy congregations responded to the tide of immigrants and the social consequences of industrialization by moving to new neighborhoods, as many downtown New York churches did in moving uptown. The old-line denominations were shaken by evangelists like Dwight L. Moody who called for an activist church that would help the poor and build community. The beginnings of Protestant social work in America could be traced to one of the earliest of New York's urban missions, founded in 1855 by Presbyterian minister Lewis M. Pease and others. The nondenominational "Five Points Mission and House of Industry" provided a home for working girls (and was thus a forerunner of the YWCA) and seven buildings for welfare work, mostly meant to serve the needs of women and children.[19] The expansion of the church's role in social work was propelled by the Social Gospel, which was directed by people, mostly ministers and women, of the Goodriches' social class and background. They were New England Protestants who

approached the problem of evil with a mixture of Puritan and humanitarian principles. The essence of Puritanism . . . was "intense moral zeal both for one's own salvation and for that of the community" [Arthur Schlesinger]. The core of secular humanitarianism . . . was unquestioned trust in human capacity to practice the Judeo-Christian ethic of human brotherhood. Together the moral duty of Puritanism and the optimistic faith of humanitarianism added up to the one idea of working for God by creating a society that would prevent evil and bring out the good in man. This is the life principle of the Social Gospel.[20]

"Of Cleveland Presbyterianism," local historian A. C. Ludlow wrote, "it may be said that it was from the beginning New Englandized. In type of theological belief, then, it has always been fairly liberal, but at the same time evangelical and fairly aggressive, as seen in its missionary spirit."[21]

Cleveland was an important national center of the movement that transformed Protestant churches into headquarters for social service. An alliance of women and clergymen gave rise to a number of national organizations in the postwar period. The U.S. Sanitary Commission disbanded in the spring of 1865, but that autumn its veterans met in Cleveland in a spirit of nondenominational committment to "aggressive Christian efforts. . . . We have fallen away from the simplicity and entire consecration of the early Christians. At first, every disciple was a missionary and every church a missionary society."[22] A report on mission work in cities was commissioned, and its publication in 1867 declared that "no mission field is more necessitous, none more easily accessible, none which appeals to so many interests of the Christian patriot and philanthropist as this in our very midst."[23] The Old Stone Church became, in the late 1860s and early 1870s, a hub of social service activities in which women played major roles.[24] If "aggressive" Christianity was the first principle of the Christian Commission, a second principle was utilization of women in the work. Sisterhoods and orders of deaconesses were suggested in 1868, and the "theory that woman has no place in the Church" was denounced as having deprived America of "two-thirds of its Christian force."[25] Cleveland's active YWCA, strongly supported by The Old Stone Church, established a home for fallen women in 1868, soon followed by a day nursery and kindergarten. The Women's Christian Temperance Union (WCTU) grew out of a local Cleveland crusade, and the national organization was formed there in 1874.

William Henry Goodrich was an influential leader, known beyond his own city for, among other talents, his literate, reasoned, and at times poetic preaching. In William's view of "the worlds," there was boundless optimism. In recent history, he saw God's triumph over slavery as a vindication of the assumptions of his class and region. In recent scientific discoveries, which some clergymen found blasphemous, Goodrich saw God's handiwork as a puzzle that could be solved by educated people, and was proof of God's power. In everything, he saw the underlying progress of America toward near-perfection. In a sermon (privately published before 1872), William's Romantic view of "The Mountains" is similar to Wordsworth's or Byron's: "No one of us probably, has ever passed from the tameness of a level land to the presence of great mountain ranges without being conscious of a positive elevation of his nature."[26] William finds no threat in Darwin or the geologists, noting that it is from mountains that "we derive the main facts on which our knowledge of God's creative work is based. He left this wondrous record of ancient convulsions, of long cycles of extinct life, graven in the rocks that man might at last read it, at least by some dim signs. He tore open to our view these leaves of the book of nature, these vivid traces and fragments of a perished world, cast in stone, that we might stand in awe of Him whose boundless resource they only hint at."[27] He acknowledges that "subjects such as those which I have lately brought before you are exceptional in the pulpit. Nor do they admit of formal application," but William is exhorting his listeners to a greater appreciation of "God's Handiwork": "It is a poor Christianity which can see God only through a beaten way of doctrines and ordinances. The Gospel is no less dear, the atonement no less precious, when we recognize our Lord not only as He hangs upon the cross, but also as He that made the worlds."[28]

Perhaps of most interest in William Goodrich's sermon – in light of his daughter's later work in Appalachia – is one of the early published comments on southern mountain people that distinguishes them from other southerners:

Explain it how we may, there belongs, in fact, to mountain regions a moral elevation of their own. They give birth to strong, free, pure and noble races. They lift the men who dwell among them, in thought and resolve. Slavery, falsehood, base compliance, luxury, belong to the plains. Freedom, truth, hardy sacrifice, simple honor, to the highlands. It is so in the old world, where one genuine republic has stood undisturbed for centuries, and looked down from its cliffs on all the varying tide of dynasties and empires; and where, for ages beyond reckoning, the Vaudois peasants have kept, above all the surging flood of Romish superstition, the faith once delivered to the saints. It was so in this land, where, in the great rebellion, the mountains of Georgia and Tennessee preserved a band of unchanged patriots, who had never stooped to share the great iniquity framed all around them into law.

By what process these loftier traits are wrought in dwellers in the mountains, the world over, it is perhaps impossible to tell. It may be due in part to a scattered, often a solitary life, sheltered from the worst temptations of a thronged society. Sin dreads solitude and hides its individuality in crowds. But the same conditions exist in other places of the earth without the same result. We must believe there is something in the very presence of these grandest of God's works which sobers and enobles man.[29]

The proliferation of social service organizations and the growth of the church increased William Goodrich's workload and responsibilities even as his health deteriorated. In 1872, Frances was sixteen and making plans to attend Vassar, when her father's condition worsened and his doctor ordered him to suspend his duties at the church and seek a rest cure. The family packed quickly and departed for Europe. Not surprisingly, their destination was the Alps. In the mountains, William had preached, "all things stand fresh from the hands of God. From such better atmosphere of the hills, our centers of enterprise are refreshed with a new and energetic life, and thither those worn with the toil and crowd of cities, go to recreate lost strength and borrow fresh vigor."[30] The Goodriches travelled in England, Italy, and France before settling in Switzerland, where Frances studied French and took lessons from an English painter. William was attended by private physicians in a Swiss clinic, but even in the Alps the "fresh vigor" he sought eluded him. In 1874, the Reverend William Goodrich died in Lausanne and the family returned to Cleveland.

They stayed two years in Ohio, seeing to financial affairs, and by 1876 they had returned to the Goodrich hometown of New Haven, Connecticut.[31] One reason for their return was probably to be nearer to their large extended family in New England, and another was that the children were of, or approaching, college age. It was probably ordained from his birth in 1864 that Chauncy William, only son of William Henry Goodrich, would someday attend Yale, as four generations of Goodrich men had done. Frances, too, attended Yale.

Under the tutelage of an English watercolorist, Frances had shown considerable artistic promise. Education for women (especially of Frances' social class) was a powerful new force in society, but few professions lay open to the educated woman. Among those that were available and acceptable were education, religious or social service, and art. In her career, Frances Goodrich was to combine aspects of each. Her college training consisted of four years (1879–1882) at the Yale School of Fine Arts. Among girls of her social class, Frances' talent may have been exceptional, but her artistic inclinations were typical. Isabell Anscombe has pointed out that these "daughters of Puritan families" before the Civil War had been

as the novelist Edith Wharton observed, a "'toast' and little else. . . . 'The ladies, God bless 'em' sums it up." But the years after the Civil War saw the gradual beginning of social change. Foreign travel became more common. . . . In America European tutors and governesses were plentiful and, as a new middle class emerged, it began to model itself on European fashions. In the home, skills such as embroidery gave way to music; novels, formerly banned as "untrue," became acceptable reading for young ladies; women learned to paint, often taking lessons while in France or Germany.[32]

The Yale School of Fine Arts was the first art school at an American university, and the first part of Yale to admit women. The course of study emphasized studio drawing and painting based on the human form. Lectures were given on perspective and anatomy, and students were required to attend lectures on the history and philosophy of art with "photographic examples of painting, sculpture and architecture thrown upon the screen by the calcium light."[33] In her later career, painting became more of a hobby than a profession for Frances Goodrich, but the obligatory lectures on history and philosophy of art doubtless played a role in her later interest in handicrafts. She was very well aware of the currents of thought emanating from followers of John Ruskin and William Morris, which were stimulating a greater interest in crafts and would give rise to the social settlement movement. Ruskin "advanced a Romantic critique of industrialism by analyzing the relation of art to labor and the relationship of both to the human soul."[34] The Art School's own building was a Venetian Gothic structure designed by a follower of Ruskin. Women students, then a novelty in New Haven, were allowed to attend because Augustus Russell Street, who endowed the School, insisted that it be open to both sexes. The University, however, would not award degrees to women students, who instead received only certificates of attendance.[35]

After her study at Yale, Goodrich went to New York to be an artist.[36] Exactly when she moved to New York, or how long she stayed, is not known. She studied with George H. Smillie, a well-known landscape artist, who was a friend of John F. Weir, the director of the Yale School of Fine Arts and Goodrich's professor of painting. Her work gained some recognition in New York, including the showing of at least one painting in an exhibition sponsored by the prestigious American Watercolor Society. Sometime in the 1880s, she and Julia briefly visited Colorado. Little is known of her life from 1882 to 1890, but it is difficult to imagine that she would have abandoned her involvement in church and in social service organizations (such as the YWCA), which began in Cleveland and continued through all other periods of her life.

Sometime in the late 1880s, she determined that the artist's life was not satisfactory for her. In the spring of 1890, she travelled for the first time to Asheville, North Carolina, where she was the guest of Florence Stephenson, who had also been in New York until 1887, studying at the New York City Mission Training School and the Industrial Education Association.[37] Stephenson and Goodrich may have met in church and social service circles in New York before Stephenson left for Asheville to run the Home Industrial School.

The question of what changed Frances Goodrich's career plans from art to social service is perhaps hinted at in a fictionalized account written by Goodrich years later, which clearly shows that Goodrich thought of the Appalachian work as an extension of the urban social settlement movement.[38] In the story, the autobiographical character is described as

a missionary; that is, she lives the kind of life a Christian woman ought to live, and she lives it among people who haven't so much to help them to be good as the people of–well, let us say Boston. . . . It was she who spoke now. "Did I ever tell you what the one thing was that sent me to the Southern mountains? If the schools of Persimmon Valley are worth anything, they are a case in point. Years ago before you knew me, I was spending a summer with a friend in the Adirondacks. Her cousin, a learned professor and a quiet, unassuming woman, was with us one evening, and at my friend's request she told us her plans for a settlement in one of the large cities. It was in the dawn of settlement work, and the exposition so modestly given of the idea at the root of these enterprises opened a new world to me. The searchings of heart as to what use I could be in the world resolved themselves into a plan and a purpose as we sat in the dusk and listened to the low voice of the seer of things to do and the way to do them."[39]

To Help Them to Be Good

Beyond her devotion to God and her desire to be of service, Goodrich's personal motives for entering mission work in Appalachia may never be known. As to why there was missionary work in Appalachia, the reasons are complex, but some of them may be suggested.[40] The missionary spirit in northern Protestant churches found many outlets for its zeal: foreign missions, city missions, and home missions to "exceptional populations," such as Indians, Mormons, Freedmen and, by the 1880s, mountaineers. An important goal of Yankee republicanism was the assimilation of such populations as a part of achieving the goal of a unified nation of like people sharing a homogeneous culture and agreeing on basic values. The people of such a nation would be hard-working Christian patriots.

The South was an obvious field for mission work, being first declared sinful and then, by its defeat in the Civil War at the hands of God's forces, proven so. During the war, northern missionaries were allowed to occupy southern churches in areas held by Union troops. Southern clergymen had lost their claim on souls by their participation in the "great iniquity." After the war, the freed slaves were identified as an "exceptional population" and, as a population rather than as individuals, were served by Congregationalists, Episcopalians, and Presbyterians from the North. By the late 1880s, some of the focus of these efforts had shifted from southern blacks to mountain whites. The early efforts in Western North Carolina had their roots in freedmen's work and in the city missions. Presbyterian minister Luke Dorland was a founder of Scotia Seminary (1872) for black girls in Concord, North Carolina, and of the Dorland Institute (1887) for mountain girls in Hot Springs, Madison County, North Carolina.[41] L. M. Pease, the pioneer missionary who started the Five Points Mission in New York City (1855), also started what became Asheville Home Industrial School for girls (1877), to which New York–trained Florence Stephenson came as principal in 1887. When Frances Goodrich visited the school's graduation in 1890, she learned from Stephenson

that the major problem was not at school but back in the mountains from which these students came. . . . "Now," Miss Stephenson told her inquirer, "do you suppose you could go into some mountain community and live there yourself, raise the standard of human life, and bring some sort of order out of chaos?"[42]

Though the larger goal of the Presbyterians was the transformation of the whole of mountain society into an assimilated, properly Christianized part of greater America, there was, in the Asheville area, a special interest in the welfare

Frances Louisa Goodrich and the "Double Bowknot" coverlet that
inspired her handicraft revival work, photographed in 1943, during the
last year of her life. (Southern Highland Handicraft Guild)

The William Leatherwood family of Haywood County,
North Carolina, about 1890. Coverlets were important to mountain
families before the handicraft revival, and many used them
as backdrops for family portraits. (Mountain Heritage Center)

Frances Goodrich collected the work of her craftspeople in a mule-drawn wagon. Very likely, the coverlets in the back were sold in such places as Ohio, Connecticut, and New Hampshire. (Frank Shelton)

Loggers arrange logs behind the splash dam on the Laurel River, about 1901. Goodrich complained to the lumber company that releases of logs destroyed footlogs and bridges, thus preventing people from attending her schools and mothers' meetings. (Frank Shelton)

Frances Louisa Goodrich, about 1890, when she began working in
the North Carolina mountains. (Author's collection)

"So the plain, neat little cottage is built." At Brittain's Cove, Buncombe County, North Carolina, Goodrich built the first of many mission stations. She thought such "model homes" would inspire the locals to replace their windowless cabins with frame houses. (Southern Highland Handicraft Guild)

"The Library," about 1894. It was probably here that the "Double Bowknot" coverlet was given to Goodrich by Mrs. Davis, and here one of the first Appalachian handicraft revival programs grew out of "mothers' meetings." (Southern Highland Handicraft Guild)

Frances Goodrich on her pony "Fleet."
(Southern Highland Handicraft Guild)

Two women winding a warp in Laurel Country,
about 1900. (Frank Shelton)

Children at one of the Laurel mission schools play "Duck-Duck-Goose"
about 1901. Though she is best known for her craftwork, the education of
children was the main purpose of Goodrich's mountain work.
(Frank Shelton)

Fleet and Aunt Fan
starting for Asheville.

The Train that took Aunt Fan
from Pulman to Asheville.

Aunt Fan shopping in Asheville

The Mule Kate that
took aunt Fan the last two
miles to Allanstand.

Aunt Fan's house at
Allanstand.

Pen-and-ink drawings by Frances Louisa Goodrich
in 1902 depict scenes from a shopping trip to Asheville.
(Author's collection)

The "Weaving Cabin" at Allanstand was the site in 1899 of the first exhibition of work by the "Allanstand Cottage Industries Guild."
(Southern Highland Handicraft Guild)

Louise Payne (left) in the yard of her home near Allanstand. She was one of the first young women to undertake learning to weave as a result of Goodrich's revival. Weaving was beginning to decline until Goodrich matched young women like Louise Payne with master weavers like Elmeda Walker. Figure on the porch is unidentified. Note spinning wheel on porch.
(Southern Highland Handicraft Guild)

Frances Goodrich warping on the side of her cottage in Holderness, New Hampshire, where she spent every summer from 1880 to 1943. (Author's collection)

'The Blue Mountain Room," Woodrow Wilson's bedroom at The White House, as redecorated by Ellen Axom Wilson in 1913. The upholstery fabric was woven by Elmeda Walker of Flag Pond, Tennessee, and the overshot rug was made by Josephine Mast of Valle Cruces, North Carolina. The rosewood bed is the famous oversized one made for Abraham Lincoln. (The White House)

Allanstand, North Carolina, about 1910, showing (left to right) Allanstand
Presbyterian Church, teachers' home, and schoolhouse. Passing through
in 1897, Goodrich noticed that the people there still wore homespun clothing
and decided this was fertile ground for her handicraft revival. With such
clusters of buildings, Goodrich hoped to emulate New England
villages and provide mountaineers with "community."
(University of North Carolina, Chapel Hill)

Carding and spinning contest
at the White Rock Fair, about 1913.
(Southern Highland Handicraft Guild)

of women and girls, and a particular dislike, on the part of the founders, for the lifestyle of mountain men. Appalachian families – men, women and children – tended their small farms and raised their animals in age-old pre-industrial patterns of hunting, fishing, gathering, making things, trading, and farming. In this pattern, L. M. Pease saw the enslavement of women by lazy men:

The men are more indolent, less ambitious and hopeful than the women. The women do the housework, milk the cows, feed the hogs; and when this is done go to the field, plough, plant, hoe and grub, as much or more than the men. I have known delicate girls and women to be hard at work in house or field, while the boys were hunting or fishing, and the husband and father had gone to the nearest town or cross-roads store with a dozen of eggs, a pound or two of butter, a couple of chickens, or a few quarts of berries which his wife and the girls had picked.[43]

The slow pace of life was especially annoying to Pease, who originally came to the mountains to regain his health after a quarter-century of living in New York:

Where idleness and indolence are honorable, and labor degrading, few will work who can possibly avoid it. And so the poor whites of the mountains have for many decades only vegetated.[44]

Pease was of the opinion that the only ones who could be truly saved were those mountaineers taken at an early age from their families and placed in boarding schools like the Home Industrial:

I am satisfied that the ordinary day schools can do but little to elevate the social and moral condition and character of the poor whites of the country. In order to do them any good they must be taken from home influences and home-formed habits and be subjected to a steady, strong and prudent discipline. Such discipline will work wonders in a few years. It will prove a mighty influence for good in remoulding the social, civil and Christian character of this mountain people.[45]

It was to the "ordinary day school" at Riceville that Frances Goodrich fotched herself to "bring order out of chaos." An anonymous writer in 1889 gave a northern Presbyterian's view of a trip to Asheville and Riceville, beginning, "A trip to Asheville in October is a delight which we wish the readers of the Home Mission Monthly could enjoy for themselves." Part of the delight, it turns out, is making cultural judgments based on the view from a train:

Leaving New York in the afternoon, passing through Washington late in the evening, the traveler will awaken the next morning in the midst of scenery not unlike that in many other sections. But one will be at once struck with the careless tillage of the land. Only small irregular portions show cultivation, and even these seem to have had indifferent care. Little ragged patches of corn and tobacco will be seen now and then about the small cabins, but the crops have a "discouraged" air. Evidently the tillers of the soil do not believe in breaking down with hard work.

The scenery, however, was inspiring and so was the Presbyterian mission work.

Well has Western North Carolina been called the "Land of the Sky." Up and up we are drawn by the straining engine, amid the gorgeous scenery of autumn, where gold and amber and tints of red abound, where everything seems to glow with an opalistic flame, from the common weed by the wayside to the loftiest peak of the circling mountains. One view vanishes behind us as another, still more entrancing, suddenly evolves itself from the near distance, until the night settles down and we emerge into an open elevated valley, encircled by the dark crests of the lofty peaks of the Blue Ridge, and Asheville is reached.

Our train was late, and it was eight o'clock when we arrived at the Home Industrial School. As our carriage halted we saw through the lighted windows which were partly open, in one of the recitation rooms a gathering of the younger pupils intently engaged in a prayer meeting. It seemed a pleasant thing that the first voice we heard as we stepped on the porch was that of a little girl reverently repeating a passage of scripture, followed by the sound of prayer by another dear child.

We paused a moment to take in the scene. The sweet voice of the teacher, the attentive posture of the children who seemed to be drinking in the words of life – outside the dark night; within light and comfort and hope: truly these young lives have been gathered into a safe, peaceful home.[46]

On one "mild autumn day," the northern visitor ventures out of Asheville to inspect the day school at Riceville, where she especially noted

our dinner in a log cabin where we were most hospitably served; . . . our visit and conference with our mission teacher – all conspired to make this trip to Riceville one long to be remembered. Here we found a good work carried on amid surroundings and difficulties which might have daunted a less devoted worker.[47]

Evangeline Gorbold, the teacher there, was, in fact, considerably daunted by Riceville, and requested that help be sent.[48] She may have been the anonymous mission teacher who wrote of her lonely situation:

Imagination could never have pictured to me the scenes through which I have passed, or my heart would have failed me before I left my home. I had no conception of such a state of society as exists here. All that woman holds dear is nothing more than a name, and to be stranded alone in such a desolate spot has sometimes almost taken my breath away. It is a wide and sad field of labor. I wish you could see some of the homes where they ask me to stay overnight. I have never seen a whole town of such forlorn wretchedness, and sometimes think polygamy is no worse than the social life here. I scarcely feel safe in the midst of it. (A companion and assistant is to be sent.—Ed.) It is worse than the pistols and murders which are at every hand, even in the stories which the children tell. . . . How long I shall be able to stand the strain I do not know. I spend some nights which are almost sleepless with the burden and responsibilities of my surroundings.[49]

The person sent by the Home Mission Board to help Evangeline Gorbold was more than a companion.

The Woman Who Runs Things

In autumn of 1890, Frances Goodrich arrived at Riceville, nine miles from Asheville, to be Evangeline Gorbold's companion and assistant. Gorbold was the teacher, Goodrich an unpaid volunteer whose duties were largely self-defined. Frances Goodrich gloried in the name given her by a local person, "the woman who runs things." Goodrich explained how day school/community work operated:

"What is the work?"
"Oh! is it *only a day school?*" Some of us have heard this so often that it seems worth-while to tell what a day school settlement in the Southern Mountains under our Woman's Board is, and what it means to the community where it is placed.

To understand the place to which the day school workers go, you must imagine a valley shut in on all sides by mountains covered with a thick growth of oak and walnut and pine. A few cabins and farm houses scattered along the road which runs through the center; not enough dwellings in sight to account for the ninety or more children said to be within reach of the proposed school, though a crowd of little faces peeps at you from every cabin door. You must climb over the mountains on either side, follow the different "prongs" of the creek, and thread many a path through the woods to the out of the way cabins before you find where all the children are to come from.

The people depend for their living chiefly upon farming, done with few appliances and little skill. Many own no land, and as renters, have a hard struggle. Sunday is ill-kept, and morals are lax. Perhaps an attempt has been made to carry on a Sunday school, but through want of interest or through neighborhood jealousies it has come to naught. The better class of people are "plumb out of heart," as they see their children growing up without education, with evil influences around them, but they are helpless without a leader.

To such a neighborhood as this, two or three women are sent, and the first thing they do is to make a home. If they try to board, even with the best of the people, they waste health and strength, and lose, besides, one of the strongest factors in their influence as an uplifting force in the community. One young woman sent alone to such a post, wrote, after two months' trial, "I shall die of remorse if I go away, and of lone-liness and dyspepsia if I stay." With the establishment of the teachers' home, we are no longer shut up to these alternatives.

So the plain, neat little cottage is built, not better than the neighbors might aspire to, if their ambition were aroused, and it becomes a refuge for the weary teachers, a model of good housekeeping, of beauty and cleanliness, and a center of help and neighborly kindness.

Then comes the day school, which continues for eight or nine months of the year, and requires one or two teachers, according to the number of scholars.

One of the missionary household has no duties in the schoolroom except in a general supervision. It would be hard to define her position more accurately than was done by a neighbor who inquired for her as "the woman who runs things." Another neighbor calls her "the busiest human on the creek," and indeed she is, for she has many "things" to run. Housekeeping in itself is not easy so many miles from supplies, but that becomes a minor matter after the other duties begin to pile up.

To her falls the greater share of the visiting, and she finds her way to homes far and near. In some of the homes there are old people, infirm or bed-ridden, to whom no preacher of the Gospel has found his way with a word of comfort, and who are most grateful for a visit and for a "good talk" and a prayer. They say it gives them something to "study on" in the long, lonely days. Some of the women are shy and suspicious, and it is some time before they give their trust to the stranger, but once gained their confidence is whole-hearted.

So many opportunities come to one who is looking for them: a simple remedy given for an ailment; nourishing food for an invalid who "cain't seem like eat the corn bread and bacon;" a hint to a wife or daughter in the care of the sick; the dressing of a bad surgical case; helping out the slender trousseau of a bride, or robing a little body for the grave in fair, white garments, which brings a little sense of comfort to the poor mother, and earns her lasting love for the one who cared for her darling.

On Sunday there is always the Sunday school and meetings of an informal kind, and once in a while a minister comes to preach.

By the work of the teachers in the school and in the homes, the ground is prepared for him and the word falls on good soil. The preaching of our Presbyterian ministers is appreciated, though so different from the exciting exhortations of the "big meetin's." Of one it was said: "He don't rant none, and he don't rave none, and he don't rare none. He just says it out plain so the young people can understand." Of another, "He don't preach nary no doctrine but the plain gospel."

As time goes on, and the minister comes more frequently, the nucleus of a church is formed, and spiritual results are seen which were scarcely dreamed of at first. Changes of character, growth in Christian virtues, results which abide, and which cannot be se-cured as some would seem to think, by a little evangelistic work, a series of meetings, an excitement and many professions, but which come as the reward of days and years of patient continuous effort both in preaching and living.

For all who are well acquainted with the mountaineers will agree that it is not teaching alone that they need, not preaching alone, but practicing—a Christianity lived out before them by both preacher and teacher.

At last those who have been working thus in a corner are surprised to find that the light kindled there has spread for miles about. For years one and another has been watching them, keeping informed of every phase of their work, and at last has pronounced it good.

Much evil remains to be conquered, but the community as a whole has been raised to a higher level, and to higher aims. Through a day school, God has wrought mighty work, and "the people that sat in darkness have seen a great light."

You will not wonder that we, who have seen this miracle, plead for more such schools, well equipped in buildings and appliances, but above all, in faithful and sensible teachers. Our boarding schools which are doing such a great work for this region, while needing extension, do not need to be multiplied, but the day schools are wanted in many and many a place where they would supplement the work of the boarding schools.[50]

In 1892, when a minister was found for Riceville, Gorbold and Goodrich moved across the mountain to Brittain's Cove. The first mission to be started by Frances Goodrich began with a day school serving 82 pupils. Near the school, a cottage named "The Sparrow's Nest" along with a smaller building known as "The Library" were built at Goodrich's expense. The Library was used for "mothers' meetings, sewing meetings, Bible and cooking lessons."[51]

The Brittain's Cove mission, according to Presbyterian accounts, was widely accepted by the local people. The school was overflowing—instead of the 40 students they had been told to expect, over 80 were attending. In fall of 1895, Goodrich started a Sunday school in The Library. The Reverend I. H. Polhemus, the travelling preacher who served Brittain's Cove reported that

The whole community, with the exception of three families, rallied to The Library, and from that moment a spirit of concord and good will has ruled in the place. It was a marvellous change, for it was done after much prayer, and under the Spirit's direction.

Then last winter, a poor man, who lived far up the Cove, whose cabin could only be reached by the roughest of mountain paths, and a climb that taxed my full strength, hurt his foot, which got into a terrible condition, with five open sores, and blood-poisoning. He suffered intensely, and the neighbors could do nothing for him. Miss Goodrich undertook to care for him, and every day for weeks, in sunshine and in storm, over brooks swollen with rains, and roads covered with mud and snow, she went to him, dressed his foot, and ministered to him, until the disease was checked and his life was spared. Such heroic and loving service is seldom given in these mountains, and has gained for Miss Goodrich the love and reverence of all the community, and of many far beyond who have not seen her face. That Christ-like devotion did much to strengthen, establish and settle the work she was doing. The mothers' meetings, and the Sunday school and Church services were all blessed, because something of that same spirit came into them, and the people began to realize and recognize the presence of God.[52]

In addition to the saintly work she was doing, Goodrich's efforts were staving off competing missionaries. Two Mormons reportedly passed Brittain's Cove without proselytizing there "because it was too Presbyterian."[53]

In December 1986, the Brittain's Cove Presbyterian Church was dedicated. Built largely by contributions Goodrich had arranged in Binghamton and Cleveland, the church bore a plaque in memory of William Henry Goodrich.

An Old Brown Coverlet

It was the mothers' meetings in The Library that led to Frances Goodrich's craft program. In a fictionalized description of a mothers' meeting, Goodrich's characters sew on a quilt, exchange news ("They broke up the still and took Billy off") and talk about the positive changes brought by the missionaries:

"Why to go along this creek on Sundays it used to be just scandalous," said Alvira. "Boys pitching quoits and picking the banjo and playing cards, and kicking up all kinds of devilment; anyone to have rid through here then would have said it was plumb like a grocery. . . . There are several that were powerful rowdy and wild when the school first come in here that have calmed down mightily.[54]

It was probably to a mothers' meeting that one of the local women brought the famous Double Bowknot coverlet. In *Mountain Homespun,* Goodrich does not name the coverlet donor, identifying her only as one of the "neighbor women." In her earliest published rendering of the story, the 1902 brochure for Allanstand Cottage Industries, Goodrich wrote:

The two or three women who made a home together in the little cottage near the schoolhouse found many avenues of approach to their neighbors, but a problem faced them such as meets every one who sets himself to social service, namely, how to bring material help to the poorer among these neighbors without hampering them, or injuring their self-respect. It was through a gift from a well-to-do woman in the Cove that the end of a clew was found which has led to a partial solution. This gift was a home-woven coverlet, forty years old, slightly faded, but still beautiful in its golden brown and cream white hues.[55]

The last version of the story written by Goodrich in 1938 begins:

"I've brought you a present, knowing that you take delight in such as this." So said Mrs. D. of Brittain's Cove. She was carrying a large white poke and from it she pulled, to my astonished and admiring gaze, an old coverlet, brown and white, woven by her sister. The pattern was the "Double Bowknot" and the brown wool was dyed with chestnut-oak bark. With the spread she brought me the "draft" by which it had been woven.[56]

A photograph of the original draft is reproduced on page 9 of *Mountain Homespun*. A copy of the draft is in the collection of the Southern Highland Handicraft Guild, where Frances Goodrich's handwriting identifies it as the draft "given FLG by Mrs. William Davis of Brittain's Cove with the Old Brown Coverlet which is colored with Chestnut Oak Bark." Frances Goodrich's accounts of the coverlet do not agree on the date of the gift. A December 1901 article quotes Goodrich as saying "about nine years ago," which would make the date of the gift about 1892; *Mountain Homespun* (p. 21) says "in the year 1895," and Goodrich's' 1938 telling gives the date as 1894.[57]

In calling Mrs. William Davis "a well-to-do" woman, Goodrich was not implying that she was fabulously wealthy, but rather that she was not extremely poor and belonged to the upper of two classes of mountaineers that the missionaries believed to exist. An orientation booklet given to newly arrived mountain missionaries gives this brief guide to mountaineer-spotting:

Within this district are found two classes of people, and there is lacking that public spirit and common interest which weld together other communities of our country. One class is the cultivated and intelligent people living on the fertile farms and in villages in the valleys, and the other numbering between one and two millions dwelling in the mountain districts. Superficial observers get entirely opposite views of the characteristics and the needs of the people of this section. If one travels in the valleys only, he sees that, simply by the exercise of more thrift and energy, the institutions of church and school could soon be made equal to any in our land; and, providing his route has kept him only in the mountain districts, he is overwhelmed to find his own race and nation so sorely in need of educational advantages, so poorly housed, so bound by poverty, so regardless or so hopeless concerning the future welfare of their children.[58]

Inspired as she was by the coverlet, it was not coverlets that first occupied Goodrich's mothers' meetings–turned–craft program. Four-harness overshot coverlet weaving was too difficult for novices. The first project was wall-hangings made from scraps of silk sent from the North. Such rag weaving was a standard activity at northern urban settlements like Hull House in Chicago. The end product, made from the cast-offs of northern church women, could even be sold up north, but such sales were disguised charity. Goodrich wanted products that would be bought for their intrinsic value.

The old draft Mrs. Davis had given her intrigued Goodrich, who wondered if it could be deciphered and the coverlet reproduced. The coverlet itself "made a journey north and the admiration it received made me believe that if we in the cove could produce the like, a market could be found."[59] Indeed, Frances Goodrich knew that an admiration for such coverlets already existed in the North. Old-time domestic weaving had disappeared in New England by the time of the Civil War, and as early as 1864, coverlets were being used in "historical" displays to evoke nostalgic and patriotic images of America's past. At the "Sanitary Fairs" held in Brooklyn, Manhattan, Poughkeepsie, St. Louis, Philadelphia, and Indianapolis to raise money for war relief work, the most popular attractions were the "Colonial Kitchens," early "living history" attractions complete with costumed spinner and coverlets on view. A similar kitchen was a hit at the International Centennial Exposition at Philadelphia in 1876. Nearby, the Centennial Exposition's painting exhibition was dominated by "Colonial" interiors. In many of the paintings, selected by Yale Art School director John F. Weir (soon to be Goodrich's professor), the colonial woman is shown surrounded by the products of her home loom. By 1880, Deerfield Academy in Massachusetts opened one of the first "period rooms," which contained an old-fashioned bed with a hand-woven straight-seam coverlet. From such influences had developed by 1890 a "Colonial Revival" in architecture and the decorative arts.[60] It was not as Appalachian folk art that Goodrich first envisioned the market for coverlets, but as reproductions of New England antiques.

"Did I hold the clue to my puzzle in my very hand?" Frances Goodrich asked herself about the Double Bowknot. The drama with which she imbues the scene implies that it was the first moment at which the union of social work and handicrafts had ever been contemplated. It was, perhaps, the first beginning of that union in the Southern Appalachians, but significant precedents, almost certainly known to Goodrich, had taken place in Europe and America. In England, interest in preindustrial crafts and social work were united in the person and works of John Ruskin. The first social settlement (which depended on upper-class youths living "among" the poor, thereby providing not only advice and education, but an example of manners and good taste) was started in the London slums by Oxford and Cambridge Ruskinians in 1884. Meanwhile, in the Lake District of northern England, Ruskin was deeply involved in an attempt to help the rural poor in Langdale by reviving the handmade linen industry that had been a recent victim of industrialization. At America's best-known settlement, Jane Addams as early as 1889 was encouraging immigrants in the neighborhood of Chicago's Hull House to make craft items from the old country, which she would help to market.

In Brittain's Cove, weaving was in a state of decline. One disused loom was found in a barn, but none of the younger women knew how to weave. Gradually, Goodrich located older women who had the skills she sought. Someone's "Aunt Jane" was found who could weave plain cloth. Mrs. G.'s Aunt Sallie knew how to wind a warp. Mrs. W.'s mother-in-law was brought in to demonstrate indigo dyeing with the "blue pot." Finally the prepared yarn was taken to the Angel family on the Paint Fork of Ivy, where the women made it into three coverlets, delivered in three weeks. The coverlets were quickly sold and the southern mountain handicraft revival was underway.[61]

The Presbyterian Pup

In May 1897, Goodrich and a group of preachers rode to Greeneville, Tennessee, to attend a Presbytery meeting, passing through Allanstand, North Carolina, formerly a drover's stop on the Buncombe Turnpike. On the return trip, one of the preachers agreed to preach there, and the party joined in singing, Sunday school, and services. Goodrich was quite taken with the "Laurel Country" and declared "the time is ripe now for the day school work."[62] Goodrich had heard from others that "you may know the Laurel folk by the red," and her first view of a group of them at Allanstand confirmed that red shirts and dresses of homespun were worn by most of the people. Clearly, this spot — far from the railroad and much less accessible than Brittain's Cove — was a place where "more of the thrifty old-time ways had been kept."[63] It may have been partly this evidence of weavers nearby that persuaded Goodrich to recommend to the Board that Allanstand be the next mission station. To finance the work, Goodrich went on fund-raising trips to the north, probably taking the old Double Bowknot coverlet with her, and secured contributions sufficient to be able to say in October 1897, "with the prayers of God's people here and in the north we trust that we may go in the strength of the Lord and take possession of Allanstand for Him."[64]

Before the end of 1897, the Allanstand school was in operation and the "cottage," a substantial two-story house, had been constructed by an Asheville builder, who had to haul "all the brick, lime, nails and dressed lumber" over an "apology for a road."[65] When newly built, the house "seemed very spacious to us, but it was not long before the growing interests filled every corner, and we were put to it to find place for the materials used in the weaving industries."[66] Rather than engage the city builder again to make the needed space, Goodrich decided to have local men build a small log cabin, which was occupied by spring of 1899. A year later, another cabin, slightly larger, was built next to it and joined by a "dog-trot"—a roofed open space between them. It was in this cabin that the first exhibition of crafts was held by the "Cottage Industries Guild" in spring of 1899: "A committee of women worked hard, draping the walls with coverlets and mats, and arranging samples of women's work of many kinds; and after the closing exercises of the day-school, the cabins were filled with a crowd of interested neighbors."[67]

In 1898, the station at Big Laurel (also known as Wallins) was started, in 1899 another at Gahagans, followed by Shelton Laurel in 1899, Upper Shelton Laurel (Carmen) in 1900, Sodom (Revere) in 1901, Spill Corn in 1903, Rice's Cove in 1904, and White Rock in 1909.[68]

Though the "Laurel Field" was expanding and the schools were well attended, the local people were not unanimous in their approval of the missionaries. Many local people gave labor, firewood, even land to build the schools in their communities, but from the beginning, there was opposition from some in Madison County. Carrie Clarke, one of the teachers left in charge of Allanstand while Goodrich was busily establishing other missions, reported to Goodrich in 1901:

Well, Brother Gunter was there, the one who has been stirring them up at Gahagans about the Catholic book, I think. He was to preach, and the following are some of his remarks:—"You will be surprised to learn that I can't preach to you today, but instead I will direct my few weak remarks to a subject we are all interested in—hits about these Roman Catholics or Presbyterians as some calls 'em. I'm going to knock the bottom out 'em there doctrines! Just watch me tear up the stumps! I want yer all to be prayin' whilst I'm talking—prayin' the Lord will hold us back from follerin' every wind of doctrine of the devil's that's a walkin' up and down these valleys—yes and comin' into our very church houses!" (With a glare at me.) Then after a lot of palaver he continued to show how in a certain dictionary you could find that such a man had written such a creed, and traced it back to the Nicolatines in Revelations, whom Christ said he hated! He mentioned that he had a paper in his pockets showing that the Northern and Southern Presbyterian Church had gotten together to revise their *creed,* taking the bad out of both and putting it together, and this creed was one and the same with the one Nicolates wrote! He told of his Catholic book mentioning some of those horrid things you know found in books exposing Roman Catholicism, and ended up by saying, "And what does this all mean? Why are ye lettin' yourselves be led back to old Mother Rome! These Roman Catholics are amongst ye; jest sech is this 'mess' up here (pointing toward our house.) Go into their houses, *if they'll let ye!* and ye'll find they bow down to the Virgin Mary and have nuns there! And they do it all by their education. Oh, you mother, will you let your little ones be torn from ye? Oh, ye fathers," etc., etc. He went on ranting and raving and said: "Mebbe, some of 'em was in here. He didn't keer if they was."

I imagined the people were getting uncomfortable, they cast sidelong glances at me and were a little restless, but I looked him square in the face and tried not to show my boiling within,—it didn't hurt me, but I thought of some of the ignorant parents who might be influenced by him to take their children from school.

I have not told you half—he ranted on infant baptism and when he had finished, Bellman, made brave by the warming Gunter had given us, took up the strain and shook his finger in my very face, actually not two feet from me and did all but call me Satan himself! It was awful!

Everyone was staring at me by this time, and when it was over it was all I could do to talk a little while pleasantly with Mrs. Ramsay and some others as if nothing had happened. I was comforted by our Sunday school, however, we had 18, most of them had never attended before.

"The mess" aren't at all discomfited but are determined to win by love and perseverance.[69]

The "Catholic" rumor had been spread from the earliest stages of Presbyterian work in the Laurel Country "and that had created a great fear in the hearts of the people for they were as afraid of a Catholic as a bear."[70] Lillie McDevitt Clark's Missionary Baptist parents wouldn't let her participate in Presbyterian activities for two years after they came to Sodom to try to make Revere out of it, but Lillie went anyway, suffering the consequences along with a friend and a would-be Presbyterian pup:

The Freewill Baptist preacher had a little girl named Nellie and we got together and made plans to slip off and go to the Presbyterian Sunday school. As it was in the evening, we would not get caught. But there is always a little bird that carries news, so our mothers found out about it. The next time I saw Nellie, I asked her if her mother knew she had gone, and she said, yes. I asked her what her mother did to her, and she said "She whipped me, but I didn't mind her whipping me. But she whipped Sweeter, too," her little dog that went with her. I also got a whipping.[71]

In time, Lillie's mother became reassured that "it was Presbyterians," and no longer forbade associating with them. One mountain father in Upper Shelton Laurel said he didn't care what they were if they could teach his children and he would rather have his children "good Roman Catholics than Shelton Laurel drunkards."[72]

The (Log) House Beautiful

Alcohol and tobacco were the demons most often mentioned as part of the mountaineers' "evil way," that could be rectified by a combination of education, religion and "healthful interest," such as handicrafts: To Frances Goodrich, handicraft held the answer. "The question of character is so much involved in this matter of handiwork and the thrift it encourages that we feel the key to many of our problems lies in these cottage industries that have been started around our day-schools."[73] The character-building aspect of crafts was uppermost in Goodrich's mind, but she realized that the cash from the sales of crafts was of most interest to the women who produced them. At first, she was able to sell the goods through her contacts among northern church women, but as production increased, she sought to publicize the program to a wider audience and to create as much of a local market in Asheville as possible. She published accounts of the work in the Presbyterian Home Mission Monthly at first, then Pratt Institute Monthly, and newspapers like the Springfield (Massachusetts) *Daily Republican*. Her first article in a mass-market publication was in the December 1898 *House Beautiful*. At the spring Presbytery meeting of 1900, she organized the first exhibition of Allanstand crafts in Asheville, where "a number of fine specimens were gathered, of weaving, sewing and basket and hat making. There were examples of linen homespun, of old counterpanes, of old coverlets, and of the coverlet material the weaving of which we are taking so much pains to revive. To illustrate the work further, a weaver was at hand making homespun linsey on a hand-loom."[74] The Asheville shows became an annual event.

Such efforts were beginning to have an effect. Goodrich reports "searching in a large city for the home of a lady interested in the Laurel schools and was puzzled, not being sure of having the right street number, when I saw approaching me a lady with a piece of weaving called 'Missouri Trouble' on her arm. It was unmistakable, not only was it homespun but made by one of our weavers. . . . And it was indeed carried by the lady I sought, returning from a meeting where the 'Missouri Trouble' had been exhibited. This use for homespun, to introduce would-be friends, was one we had not reckoned on."[75]

By 1902, the log cabin at Allanstand had become a salesroom for crafts products, and the scene of at least some of the weaving. By this time, the Arts and Crafts Movement, originally inspired by Ruskin and Morris, had become a force in American decorating. As the American Arts and Crafts Movement grew, Goodrich was careful to see that Allanstand was part of it. As early as 1903, she was in contact with Gustav Stickley, editor of the influential *Craftsman* magazine and organizer of exhibitions around the country. In that year, Stickley personally selected the items for an Arts and Crafts Exhibition in Rochester, New York. The list of exhibitors included Berea Industries of Kentucky, the Abkanee Rug Industry of New Hampshire, Rookwood Pottery of Cincinnati,

Hull House Shops of Chicago, the Arts and Crafts Societies of Dayton, Philadelphia, and Deerfield, Massachusetts, and Allanstand.[76]

By 1904, the economic importance of crafts was recognized by the federal government. A Bureau of Labor bulletin reported on many of the Industries, including Allanstand, where Goodrich's method of organizing and payment was detailed:

The plan of supplying the materials and paying for the work on a piecework basis was adopted. For carding and spinning, the women were paid 33½ cents per pound of wool or 44 cents per pound of cotton; for dyeing, 20 cents per pound of wool or 25 to 30 cents per pound of cotton, the indigo and madder being furnished and various other dyestuffs being found in the woods; for weaving coverlets of the usual weight, 35 cents a yard; for weaving rugs (a faster process because of the double yarn), 25 cents a yard. These prices are somewhat higher than the customary rate of payment prevailing for coverlets woven for persons residing in the neighborhood, when the price for weaving was from 20 to 25 cents a yard; but the rate of pay has been further increased, especially for weaving, so that a first-class weaver now commands 40 to 45 cents a yard. This has encouraged several young women to learn the craft, two of whom are fitting themselves as teachers.[77]

During the first decade of the new century, with Asheville flourishing and the business growing, Goodrich decided to open a permanent salesroom in Western North Carolina's largest city. The Allanstand shop opened on Main Street in 1908.

One of the few independent appraisals of Allanstand Industries in the early days was made by Olive Dame Campbell during the fact-finding survey of mountain life she undertook with her husband John C. Campbell in 1909. Olive Campbell described the Madison County Allanstand:

There is a school building and a good-sized teacher's house (where Carmichels live) and across the road—a two room log cabin (one room for minister) the seat of the famous Allanstand Industries. No loom in room now—just a collection of odds and ends—a few baskets, rolls of wool, etc. Mr. C said industries had gone down and were now reviving.[78]

Perhaps Goodrich's attention was directed more toward the new shop in Asheville, but it is possible that Campbell may have been unaware of the dispersed locations of the workers. During her half-day visit to the area, Campbell also visited Louise Payne, one of the first of Goodrich's weavers, and watched her weaving a carpet at her cabin a quarter of a mile from Allanstand. Campbell also questioned the economics of the industries:

Perhaps there are 3 or 4 women around who are weaving for Miss Goodrich. There are several, I understand, in another county. A great question as to whether total profit would be $1,000 a year. Miss G. pays women $1.00 a yard for linsey—which can be bought at F.P. [Flag Pond, Tennessee] for 50¢ a yard. A questionable jump in price? Louise Payne weaves carpet at 50¢ a yard. Can do housework and weave a yd. a day. Miss G. furnishes wool. Can weave 4–5 yds linsey a day.[79]

At Flag Pond, Tennessee, four miles from Allanstand, several weavers worked for Goodrich, including Elmeda McHargue Walker, whose work, Goodrich said, "set the standard for our industries."[80] Walker also appears as "Aunt Elvira" in Goodrich's thinly fictionalized account of "The Three Gray Women" in *Mountain Homespun,* and her photograph is shown opposite page 56. In 1913, when Ellen Axom Wilson, wife of the newly-elected president, decided to redecorate Woodrow Wilson's bedroom as "The Blue Mountain Room," Mrs. Walker was chosen to weave the upholstery fabric in the "Sun, Moon and Stars" pattern. The White House endorsement of mountain crafts was the subject of many articles, bringing brief fame to Walker and increased attention to Allanstand and other mountain craft centers. It was a big forward step in Goodrich's efforts to create a national, middle-class market for handicrafts.

Building Main Street on Laurel

In the 1910s, the emphasis in mountain work shifted from providing schools, which were being supplied by local public school systems, to "building community."[81] In a sense, the shift was a vindication of Frances Goodrich's work. She (and her fellow day-schoolers in the field) had been busy creating not only the idea of community, through mothers' meetings and craft work, but the actual appearance in the Laurel country of "communities"—little clusters of buildings at the confluence of several streams where a school, community building, church, and at least one neat, New England–style dwelling house were grouped around a common, where special events, like a village fair, could be held. At White Rock, which Goodrich proudly called the "Keystone" station (not entirely for its Pennsylvania donors) the twenty-bed hospital opened in May 1919 announced to all: This is Main Street, Laurel, North Carolina.

If building "community" depends on assembling the participants, the White Rock Fairs have to be considered as historic steps. According to some who attended, the Fairs saw the largest single gatherings in Laurel history. In addition to the judging of canned good and cakes, there were the annual results of the work of the "Corn Clubs," a Presbyterian-encouraged grouping of men who met to upgrade their seed corn, and there were handicraft displays and carding and spinning contests. Like the schools, the fairs were replaced by local institu-

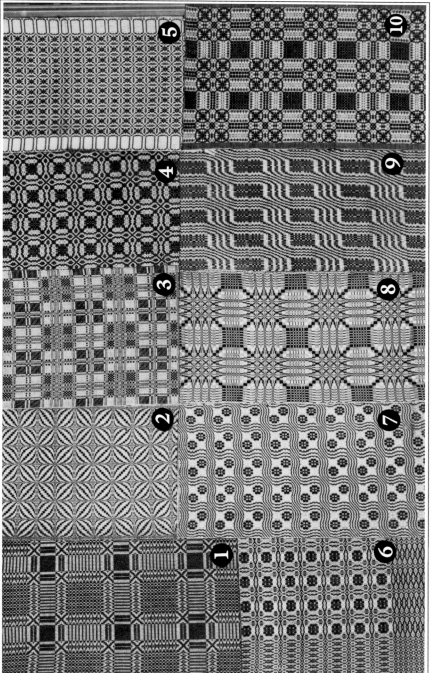

Coverlet patterns available from the Southern Highland Handicraft Guild's "Allanstand" shop in the late 1930s: (1) St. Anne's Robe, (2) Blooming Flower, (3) High Crick's Delight, (4) Zion Rose, (5) Dogwood, (6) Whig Rose with Dogwood Border, (7) Rattlesnake and Cat Tracks, (8) Pine Burr, (9) Three Roads Trail (10) Double Chariot Wheel. (Author's collection)

You are invited to meet

Miss Frances Goodrich

of the Allanstand Cottage Industries

and to attend an exhibition and sale
of the work of the Southern Mountaineers

at the residence of
Mr. Samuel Mather
2605 Euclid Avenue

on Monday, November the twenty-fourth
Nine-thirty to five o'clock

*Miss Goodrich will give a short
talk at four-fifteen, followed by tea*

PATRONESSES

Mrs. Robert H. Bishop	Mrs. Frederick W. Hitchings
Mrs. Martyn Bonnell	Mrs. Evan H. Hopkins
Mrs. W. P. Champney	Mrs. H. W. Judd
Mrs. Charles Long Cutter	Mrs. B. L. Millikin
Miss Annie S. Cutter	Mrs. Charles A. Nicola
Miss Jessica A. Eyears	Mrs. Francis F. Prentiss
Mrs. James N. Fleming	Mrs. Samuel A. Raymond
Mrs. Perry Harvey	Miss Carrie B. Smith
Miss Emily Harvey	Mrs. J. J. Tracy
Miss Ursula A. Herrick	Mrs. Edward M. Williams

Goodrich sold crafts at tea parties given by wealthy patrons.
The Mathers of Cleveland hosted this 1930 affair. (Author's collection)

Wool processes: Shearing sheep and washing wool.
(Olive Dame Campbell's photo album. Southern Historical
Collection, University of North Carolina at Chapel Hill)

Wool processes: Drying and carding wool.
(Olive Dame Campbell's photo album. Southern Historical
Collection, University of North Carolina at Chapel Hill)

Wool processes: Spinning wool and winding skeins.
(Olive Dame Campbell's photo album. Southern Historical
Collection, University of North Carolina at Chapel Hill)

Frances (right) in academic garb after being named honorary doctor
of humanities by The College of Wooster (Ohio). With her are sister Julia
and brother Chauncey Goodrich. (Author's collection)

tions, and the White Rock Fair was eventually merged into the new Madison County Fair at Marshall.[82]

White Rock and other mission stations on Laurel were important points of entry into mountain culture for outsiders, including Cecil Sharp, the English ballad-hunter who used the Presbyterian network for food and lodging while searching for songs in Madison County. In 1916 missionaries at Carmen, White Rock, and other stations introduced him to potential singers in the neighborhood. Sharp found the old English ballads he had hoped were there, and appreciated the Presbyterians' hospitality, but he was dubious about the cultural effect of the missionary work:

Some of the women [missionaries] I have met are very nice and broadminded. But I don't think any of them realize that the people they are here to improve are in many respects far more cultivated than their would-be instructors, even if they cannot read or write. Take music for example. Their own is pure and lovely. The hymns that these missionaries teach them are musical and literary garbage. . . . The problem, I know, is a very difficult one. For my part, I would leave them as they are and not meddle. They are happy, contented, live simply and healthily, and I am not at all sure that any of us can introduce them to anything better than this.

Help them with farming, perhaps, Sharp advised, and teach them to read and write. "Beyond this," he said, "I should not go."[83]

In 1913, the Presbyterian day schools were turned over to local communities and many became public schools, but the network of mission stations in Laurel remained as centers for community work. By 1916, Frances Goodrich was raising money for the White Rock Hospital (Dr. Packard was already treating patients in Laurel) and planning for her retirement from the field. The Allanstand Cottage Industries, in its twenty-one year history, had been always Goodrich's own private philanthropic business, and never officially connected with the Presbyterian Church. It existed only because of her, and she began to plan for its continuity after she was unable personally to run it.

In January 1917, it became Allanstand Cottage Industries, Incorporated, with shares available at $25. Article VII of the bylaws read:

The aim of the corporation is to help the people of the Southern Highlands to produce and to market handiwork, especially handwoven articles, basketry and woodwork, and by so doing, to bring money into communities far from markets, and to give paying work to members of such communities; to give to the workers the interest of producing beautiful things, the delight of the skilled worker and artist; to save from extinction and to develop the old-time crafts of the mountains.[84]

The incorporation may have been at least partly responsible for an increase in sales from $4,776 in 1916,[85] to $10,000 in 1918[86] and $16,000 in 1921.[87]

When she "retired" in 1918, Goodrich permanently transferred her headquarters to 89 Victoria Road, Asheville, but did not slow down her busy patterns of activity. The home she shared with her sister, Julia, was a small, two-story "craftsman" bungalow of dark brick across the street from Asheville's complex of Presbyterian schools: the Asheville Home Industrial School, Asheville Normal, and the Pease House for Girls. At these institutions, at the Asheville Farm School ten miles away, at Dorland-Bell School in Hot Springs, and at every mission station in Laurel, the Goodriches were conspicuous visitors and active participants. They advised students, spoke to classes, and taught songs to the little children. Older girls from the schools across the road honed their social skills taking tea with the Goodriches.

The Godmother

As President of the Allanstand Corporation, Frances Goodrich continued to be involved in every aspect of the craft business, from taking a turn keeping the shop, to organizing exhibitions and writing publicity. The publicity changed from the judgmental paternalism (or is it properly maternalism?) of 1898 to the more egalitarian tone of the 1920s. World War I, in which mountain people like the famous Sergeant Alvin C. York shared equally in the sacrifices, helped make it unfashionable, even among those writing charitable appeals, to blame the victims for their troubles. In 1898, Goodrich expressed the goal of Allanstand as "the gain in habits of industry and thrift," adding that "it is in great measure the loss of these qualities that has caused the mountaineers to fall behind in the race."[88] In 1922 the goal was to give the workers "a new interest, the pleasure of producing beautiful things, the delight of the skilled worker and artist. With this comes a consciousness of the brotherhood of labor which relieves the monotony and sordidness of life. Habits of thrift, of keeping work up to a standard, are fostered, tending directly to the building of character."[89]

Craft programs, some with stories similar to Allanstand's, multiplied in the 1920s in Western North Carolina. Olive Dame Campbell started the John C. Campbell Folk School in Brasstown in 1925, based on Danish models, and with a strong emphasis on crafts.[90] Lucy Morgan, a mountain native, started a "Fireside Industries" at an Episcopal school in Penland that by the end of the decade had become the Penland School of Crafts. Morgan brought in Edward F. Worst of Chicago, the country's best-known authority on handweaving, to supervise the summer instruction of weaving. The reputation of such famous teachers helped bring in students, not only from Mitchell and Yancey Counties, but from New York, Illinois, and California. From 1895 to the end of the 1920s, Appalachia had gone from a place where "Colonial" domestic weaving existed in a vestigial survival, to the place in America where a student of any cultural background might choose to go to learn how to be a master weaver in an increasingly international style. A process was in motion that turned a folk cultural art into a profession and a pastime.

By the late 1920s the older women who had taught Goodrich about weaving and made it possible for her to start her program were going. Elmeda Walker and all of the weaving Angels were gone. It was partly to commemorate their generation that Goodrich began to write *Homespun*. It was as a seventy-two-year-old that she began to write about the beginnings, when she was thirty-three to forty-three years old.

Late in 1928, several of her fellow craft organizers met at the Weaver's Cabin in Penland to start forming a "guild." Although Goodrich did not make the rough trip in snowy weather, she sent a message of support, and may have stayed home working on the manuscript of *Homespun*. Early in 1929, she contacted her cousin, Mrs. Alfred Bacon of New Haven, and told her about the memoir she was writing, perhaps suggesting that Mrs. Bacon mention it to her good friend, the co-founder of the Yale University Press, Wilhelmine Day. Mrs. Day read the manuscript, liked it, recommended it to her husband, Yale Press director George P. Day, and the Press decided to publish it. Goodrich sent photographs for illustrations, retrieving one of the Double Bowknot that showed the wrong side of the coverlet and replacing it with a correct one. On September 18, when publication seemed imminent, Goodrich wrote Yale University Press editor Malcolm W. Davis:

I should very much like to have an interview with the one on your staff responsible for notices, to say a word of warning as to what not to say about the mountaineers and my connection with them. A word or phrase may give offence and one has to live among them to find these out.[91]

Worrying about illustrations and offensive blurbs, however, was premature. The stock market crash of October 29 threw every business decision into doubtful status. Nevertheless, nineteen days later, George P. Day approved securing an estimate for *Homespun*.

On December 29, when she attended the official formation meeting of the "Southern Mountain Handicraft Guild" at the Spinning Wheel in Asheville, Goodrich still had no firm publication date to announce. When the Guild held its first exposition of crafts in Knoxville in March 1930, she had been told by Davis that she could assure her colleagues that the book would be ready "next autumn." But in June, the estimate for production reached Davis, who looked it over and drew a large "x" through the figures. *Homespun,* envisioned as a grand book, was scratched until a new design could be made. A depression version—with fewer illustrations, uncoated paper, and covers of board, not vellum—was designed and a decision was made that the book was important enough to be subsidized by one of Yale's publication funds. In July, however, Goodrich got a disappointing message from Davis:

The general business depression which has adversely affected the book trade and which we have consequently felt as all other publishers have, compelled us to postpone from this autumn until next spring, about a dozen titles.[92]

The publication fund chosen to subsidize Goodrich's book was one established in memory of Amasa Stone Mather, whose mother Flora had been Goodrich's childhood friend in the Cleveland playhouse with the tiny wood-burning cookstove. In October 1930, Goodrich discovered that there was another book named *Homespun,* and decided to rename hers *Mountain Homespun.*

Assured of a spring publication for the book, Goodrich now moved on to the second part of her plan to provide for posterity. Near the end of February 1931, Goodrich assembled Clementine Douglas of the Spinning Wheel and Marguerite Bidstrup and Olive Campbell, founders of the Campbell Folk School, and laid out to them a plan for giving the whole Allanstand business to the Guild.[93]

When the Guild held its spring meeting in 1931, the business meeting was notable for the announcement of Goodrich's plan to turn over to the fledgling organization the best-known retail craft shop in the mountains. Its thirty-four-year-old reputation for quality and honesty, as well as its "surplus, consisting of stock, cash, and goodwill was given outright to this newly formed Guild."[94] The other notable event at the meeting was the first appearance of *Mountain Homespun,* which provided the newly-given Allanstand with its most valuable asset: its legend.

Mountain Homespun's central dramatic incident, the gift of the Double Bowknot, caught the attention of feature writers, who retold it frequently and compared that gift to the gift of Allanstand, thus making the blessing of the Guild the final step in conferring the management of crafts from the family, to the individual saintly woman, to a corporation directed by northerners, to a coalition with other production centers.

The New York Times reviewer thought *Mountain Homespun* "beautifully made," praised its narrative quality as "piquant" and "delightful," found its appendix of dye plants noteworthy, and said of Part II, "The People":

A charming human interest is given to the book by a series of seven sketches of mountain women of fine, capable, kindly character and their lives. This series makes a good and just antidote to all the tales of blood feuds, murders and moonshining that have won so much attention that they have colored the general conception throughout the North of mountain life and character.[95]

In the troubled 1930s the institutions and markets Goodrich had helped to create provided more choices than would have been available otherwise. Many mountain women, faced with less cash and greatly narrowed choices, turned to their looms as a source of income. Louise Payne, for example, belonged to the family that inhabited Allanstand before Goodrich and the others came. Her family lived in the original Allan buildings and boarded the workers who came to build Goodrich's house and school. When Goodrich started craft work at Allanstand, Louise Payne had been the first to volunteer to learn. She studied with Elmeda Walker, the setter of the standard, developed great skill, and wove for Allanstand off and on for years, but was especially thankful for having the skill when her husband died in 1932 and she was left to raise six children in Depression America. She later credited weaving with having saved her family.[96]

In 1938, the College of Wooster (Ohio) made Goodrich an honorary doctor of humanities. In the 1930s and 1940s, Goodrich was an active member of the First Congregational Church, Business and Professional Woman's Club, and Current Literature Club, and took a special interest in developing a branch of the YWCA for black girls and involving it with the main branch in Asheville. She became a trustee of Asheville College (formed by the union of the Home Industrial and the Normal and Collegiate Institute).

In 1943, she was featured in a film made by the U.S. Department of Agriculture on mountain crafts. She was seated at a table, working on her collection of hundreds of old weaving drafts, with the Double Bowknot hanging behind her.

Goodrich spent the fall of 1943 reading *Paradise Lost,* Greek drama, and the Venerable Bede. In early 1944, she became ill. At her "craftsman" home, surrounded by homespun, she died in her sleep at 1:30 A.M. on February 20 at the age of 87. Earlier in the evening, she had read some in the Bible, and some of Socrates to the Young Men of Athens.

At a memorial service, Lucy Morgan called her "The Godmother to the Guild" and said, "many people can be good, but not all can be good with a twinkle." An editorial in the Asheville *Citizen* said that the mountain people "never had a more understanding or helpful friend. She never patronized or slummed among them. With their homely wisdom they taught her much for which she was ever-lastingly grateful. She taught them much for which they loved her."[97]

NOTES

1. See David E. Whisnant, *All That is Native and Fine: The Politics of Culture in an American Region* (Chapel Hill: Univ. of North Carolina Press, 1983); esp. intro. and 103–80.

2. See Curtis Wood and Joan Greene, "Origins of the Handicraft Revival in the Southern Mountains" in Helen Roseberry, ed., *Remembrance, Reunion and Revival* (Boone, NC: Appalachian Consortium Press, 1988), 108–14, and Eileen Boris, *Art and Labor: Ruskin, Morris, and the Craftsman Ideal in America* (Philadelphia: Temple Univ. Press, 1986), 122–38.

3. Ronald D Eller, *Miners, Millhands, and Mountaineers,* (Knoxville: Univ. of Tennessee Press, 1982), 124–26.

4. Manly Wade Wellman, *The Kingdom of Madison: A Southern Mountain Fastness and Its People* (Chapel Hill: Univ. of North Carolina Press, 1973), 124.

5. Frank B. Shelton and Richard Dillingham, interviews with author, Oct. 27, 1988.

6. Frances Louisa Goodrich (hereinafter cited as FLG) to Chauncey Goodrich, Feb. 9, 1901, in author's possession.

7. David E. Whisnant, "Second Level Appalachian History," *Appalachian Journal* 9, nos. 2 and 3 (Winter-Spring 1982): 155.

8. See Lillie McDevitt Clark, *Appalachian Memories* (Weaverville, NC: Reems Creek Homemakers Club, n.d.), esp. 19–21.

9. Jacqueline Burgin Painter, *The Season of Dorland-Bell: History of an Appalachian Mission School* (Asheville, NC: Biltmore Press, 1987), 4.

10. Thomas R. Dawley, *The Child That Toileth Not: The Story of a Government Investigation that was Suppressed* (New York: Gracia, 1913), 190.

11. Grover Angel, interview with author, Oct. 27, 1988.

12. FLG, "Old Ways and New in the Carolina Mountains," *Southern Workman*, April 1900, 211.

13. FLG to Chauncey Goodrich, Feb. 9, 1901.

14. Eller, 115.

15. FLG to S. F. Lincoln, Feb. 17, 1900.

16.   Goodrich genealogy, in author's possession.

17.   Discussion of childhood is based on Julia Goodrich, "Memories of Early Days in Cleveland," manuscript, Western Reserve Historical Society, Cleveland, OH.

18.   Ibid.

19.   See Aaron Ignatius Abell, *The Urban Impact on American Protestantism, 1865–1900* (Cambridge, MA: Harvard Univ. Press, 1943; rpt. New York: Archon, 1962), chaps. 1–3.

20.   Arthur Mann, *Yankee Reformers in the Urban Age* (Cambridge, MA: Belknap Press of Harvard Univ. Press, 1954), 73.

21.   Arthur Clyde Ludlow, *History of Cleveland Presbyterianism* (Cleveland, OH: n.p., 1896), 4.

22.   Quoted in Abell, 12.

23.   Abell, 13.

24.   "The Old Stone Church," brochure, First Presbyterian Church, Cleveland, OH.

25.   Abell, 15.

26.   William Goodrich, *God's Handiwork in the Sea and the Mountains; Sermons Preached After a Summer Vacation* (Cleveland, OH: Pub. by request, n.d.), 16.

27.   Ibid., 18.

28.   Ibid., 25.

29.   Ibid., 23–24.

30.   Ibid., 23.

31.   FLG, "Accurate Sketch of the Life of Frances Louisa Goodrich," manuscript, in author's possession.

32.   Isabell Anscombe, *A Woman's Touch: Women in Design from 1860 to the Present Day* (New York: Viking, 1984), 35.

33.   "Yale School of Fine Arts," brochure, n.d.

34.   Boris, 4.

35.   Judith Ann Schiff (Chief Research Archivist, Yale University Library), May 29, 1987, to author.

36.   FLG, "Accurate Sketch."

37.   FLG, *Florence Stephenson*, 8.

38.   See Allen F. Davis, *Spearheads of Reform*, 1–11.

39.   Jane Greenleaf [FLG], *Home Mission Monthly* (hereinafter cited as *HMM*), Sept. 1909: *HMM* citations to the bound volumes at the Presbyterian Historical Society, Philadelphia, include volume, year, and page; clippings from broadside numbers of *HMM* in FLG's scrapbook (dated in her hand) are cited with month and year only.

40.   See Henry Shapiro, *Appalachia on Our Mind: The Southern Mountains and Mountaineers in the American Consciousness, 1870–1920* (Chapel Hill: Univ. of North Carolina Press, 1978), 32–58, passim.

41.   See Painter, chapters 1–3.

42.   Fred Eastman, "An Artist in Religion," *The Christian Century*, Aug. 6, 1930.

43.   *HMM* 3 (1888): 173–74.

44.   Ibid.

45.   *HMM* 3 (1889): 39.

46.   *HMM* 4 (1899): 52–53.

47.   Ibid.

48.   Records of the Women's Board of Home Missions (hereinafter cited as WBHM), Presbyterian Historical Society, Philadelphia.

49.   *HMM* 4 (1891): 112.

50.   *HMM*, Dec. 1897.

51.   WBHM records of Brittain's Cove.

52.   I. H. Polhemus to WBHM, Dec. 1896.

53.   Ibid.

54.   *HMM*, Dec. 1905.

55.   FLG, "Allanstand Cottage Industries" brochure, WBHM, New York, 1902.

56.   FLG, "Allanstand Cottage Industries," *Tar Heel Woman*, May 1938.

57.   Ibid.

58.   A. P. Harper, "The Mountain People of the South" (revised and condensed by Florence Stephenson), Women's Executive Committee of Home Missions of the Presbyterian Church, 1895.

59.   FLG, *Mountain Homespun* (hereinafter cited as *MH*), 22.

60. See Alan Axelrod, ed., *The Colonial Revival in America* (New York: Norton, 1986), esp. Rodris Roth, "The New England, or 'Old Tyme' Kitchen Exhibit at 19th Century Fairs," 159–84, and Celia Betsky, "Inside the Past: The Interior and the Colonial Revival in American Art and Literature, 1860–1914," 241–77.

61. *MH*, 23.

62. FLG to WBHM, May 1, 1897.

63. FLG, "Allanstand Cottage Industries" brochure.

64. FLG to WBHM, Oct. 16, 1897.

65. *HMM*, Dec. 1897.

66. *HMM*, Dec. 1903.

67. *HMM*, Dec. 1903.

68. WBHM records of Laurel missions.

69. Carrie Clarke to FLG, Dec. 1901. WBHM.

70. Clark, *Appalachian Memories*, 19.

71. Ibid., 21.

72. FLG to WBHM, July 17, 1899.

73. FLG to WBHM, July 7, 1900.

74. FLG to WBHM, July 7, 1900.

75. FLG to WBHM, July 7, 1900.

76. *Rochester Democrat and Chronicle*, April 8, 1903.

77. Max West, "The Revival of Handicraft in America," U.S. Bureau of Labor *Bulletin* 55 (Nov. 1904): 1578–79.

78. Olive Dame Campbell, diary entry for Feb. 18, 1909, Campbell Papers 3800, Southern Historical Collection, University of North Carolina, Chapel Hill.

79. Ibid.

80. *MH*, 24.

81. See Shapiro, 151–52.

82. WBHM records of White Rock.

83. Maud Karpeles, *Cecil Sharp: His Life and Work* (Chicago: Univ. of Chicago Press, 1967), 153.

84. "Allanstand Cottage Industries, Incorporated Exchange for Mountain Handicraft," brochure, Asheville, NC, 1917.

85. Watertown (CT) *Daily Times,* Feb. 8, 1917.

86. *HMM,* Nov. 1919.

87. Julia Goodrich [FLG], "Made in Mountain Homes," Jan. 22, 1922. In a letter to Allen Eaton, March 14, 1930, FLG says, "I wrote 'Made in Mountain Homes' (credited to Julia Goodrich)."

88. *Pratt Institute Monthly,* June 1898.

89. *Diversion,* Jan. 21, 1922.

90. See David Whisnant, *All That Is Native and Fine: The Politics of Culture in an American Region* (Chapel Hill, NC: Univ. of North Carolina Press, 1983), 103–79.

91. FLG to Malcolm W. Davis, Sept. 18, 1929.

92. Malcolm W. Davis to FLG, July 14, 1930.

93. "Address by Mrs. John C. Campbell," in *Frances Louisa Goodrich 1856–1944* (Asheville, NC: Privately printed, 1944), 36–37.

94. FLG, *Tar Heel Woman,* May 1938.

95. *New York Times,* March 8, 1931.

96. Mary Ellen Wolcott, "Mrs. Lamb, 91, Remembers When Weaving Saved Her Family," Asheville *Citizen,* Feb. 9, 1975.

97. *Frances Louisa Goodrich 1856–1944,* 38.

WORKS CITED

Abell, Aaron Ignatius. *The Urban Impact on American Protestantism, 1865–1900*. Cambridge, MA: Harvard Univ. Press, 1943; rpt. New York: Archon, 1962.

Angel, Grover. Interview with author, Mars Hill, NC, Oct. 27, 1988.

Anscombe, Isabell. *A Woman's Touch: Women in Design from 1860 to the Present Day*. New York: Viking, 1984.

Axelrod, Alan, ed. *The Colonial Revival in America*. [Pub. for Winterthur (Del.) Museum.] New York: Norton, 1986.

Boris, Eileen. *Art and Labor: Ruskin, Morris, and the Craftsman Ideal in America*. American Civilization Series, ed. Allen F. Davis. Philadelphia: Temple Univ. Press, 1986.

Campbell, Olive Dame. 1909 diary entries. Campbell Papers 3800, Southern Historical Collection, University of North Carolina, Chapel Hill.

Clark, Lillie McDevitt. *Appalachian Memories: A Simpler Time*. Weaverville, NC: Reems Creek Valley Homemakers Club, 1984.

Davis, Allen F. *Spearheads for Reform: The Social Settlements and the Progressive Movement, 1890–1914*. New York: Oxford Univ. Press, 1967.

Dawley, Thomas Robinson, Jr. *The Child That Toileth Not: The Story of a Government Investigation that Was Suppressed*. 2nd ed. New York: Gracia, 1913.

Dillingham, Richard. Interview with the author, Mars Hill, NC, Oct. 27, 1988.

Eastman, Fred. "An Artist in Religion." *The Christian Century*, Aug. 6, 1930.

Eaton, Allen H. *Handicrafts of the Southern Highlands*. New York: Russell Sage Foundation, 1937; rpt. New York: Dover, 1973.

Eller, Ronald D. *Miners, Millhands, and Mountaineers: Industrialization of the Appalachian South 1880–1930*. Twentieth-Century America series, ed. Dewey W. Grantham. Knoxville: Univ. of Tennessee Press, 1982.

Frances Louisa Goodrich 1856–1944. Asheville, NC: Privately printed, 1944.

Goodrich, Frances Louisa. "Accurate Sketch of the Life of Frances Louisa Goodrich." Typescript with handwritten notations, n.d.

———. *Allanstand Cottage Industries*. [Brochure.] New York: Women's Board of Home Missions of the Presbyterian Church in the USA, 1902; 2nd ed., 1909.

————. "Allanstand Cottage Industries." *Tar Heel Woman,* May 1938.

————. "Allanstand Cottage Industries (Incorporated) Exchange for Mountain Handicraft." Brochure. Asheville, NC: n.p., 1917.

————. *Florence Stephenson.* Biltmore, NC: Gollifox Press, 1933.

————. *Mountain Homespun.* New Haven: Yale Univ. Press, 1931.

————. "Old Ways and New in the Carolina Mountains." *The Southern Workman* [Hampton, Va.], April 1900, 8–11.

Goodrich, Julia. [Frances Louisa Goodrich] "Made in Mountain Homes." *Diversion* [Asheville], Jan. 21, 1922.

Goodrich, Julia. n.d. "Memories of Early Days in Cleveland." Manuscript, Western Reserve Historical Society, Cleveland, OH.

Goodrich, William Henry. *God's Handiwork in the Sea and the Mountains; Sermons Preached after a Summer Vacation.* Cleveland, OH: Pub. by request, n.d.

Harper, A. P., and Florence Stephenson. *The Mountain People of the South.* New York: Women's Executive Committee of Home Missions of the Presbyterian Church, 1895.

Home Mission Monthly (HMM). Bound vols. at the Presbyterian Historical Society, Philadelphia. Clippings from broadside numbers of *HMM* in FLG's scrapbook, in author's possession.

Karpeles, Maud. *Cecil Sharp: His Life and Work.* Chicago: Univ. of Chicago Press, 1967.

Lathrop, Virginia Terrell. "Southern Mountain Handicraft Guild Takes Over Cottage Industries." Asheville *Citizen,* July 5, 1931.

Ludlow, Arthur Clyde. *History of Cleveland Presbyterianism.* Cleveland: n. p., 1896.

Mann, Arthur. *Yankee Reformers in the Urban Age.* Cambridge, Mass.: Belknap Press of Harvard Univ. Press, 1954.

McMillan, Bonnell. Interview with author, Brittain's Cove, NC, Oct. 27, 1988.

Painter, Jacqueline Burgin. *The Season of Dorland-Bell: History of an Appalachian Mission School.* Asheville, NC: Biltmore Press, 1987.

Shapiro, Henry D. *Appalachia on Our Mind: The Southern Mountains and Mountaineers in the American Consciousness, 1870–1920.* Chapel Hill: Univ. of North Carolina Press, 1978.

Shelton, Frank B. Interview with author, Shelton Laurel, NC, Oct. 27, 1988.

West, Max. "The Revival of Handicraft in America." U.S. Bureau of Labor *Bulletin* 55 (Nov. 1904): 1578–79.

Wellman, Manly Wade. *The Kingdom of Madison: A Southern Mountain Fastness and its People*. Chapel Hill, NC: Univ. of North Carolina Press, 1973.

Whisnant, David E. *All That Is Native and Fine: The Politics of Culture in an American Region*. Fred W. Morrison Series in Southern Studies. Chapel Hill, NC: Univ. of North Carolina Press, 1983.

———. "Second Level Appalachian History: Another Look at Some Fotched-on Women." *Appalachian Journal* 9, nos. 2 and 3 (Winter–Spring 1982): 115–23.

Wilson, Sadye Tune, and Doris Kennedy. *Of Coverlets: The Legacies, The Weavers*. Nashville, TN: Tunstede Press, 1983.

Wood, Curtis, and Joan Greene. "Origins of the Handicraft Revival in the Southern Mountains." In *Remembrance, Reunion and Revival: Celebrating a Decade of Appalachian Studies, Proceedings of the 10th Annual Appalachian Studies Conference*, ed. Helen Roseberry. Boone, NC: Appalachian Consortium Press, 1988.

Wolcott, Mary Ellen. "Mrs. Lamb, 91, Remembers When Weaving Saved Her Family" Asheville *Citizen,* Feb. 9, 1975.

Women's Board of Home Missions (WBHM) of the Presbyterian Church in the USA. Records of Laurel Field, NC, Presbyterian Historical Society, Philadelphia, 1890–1920.

"Yale School of Fine Arts." [Brochure.] Pub. by the school, New Haven, CT, n.d.

Yale University Press. Correspondence about *Mountain Homespun,* 1929–1931. New Haven, CT.

INDEX

MOUNTAIN HOMESPUN

MOUNTAIN HOMESPUN

BY

FRANCES LOUISA GOODRICH

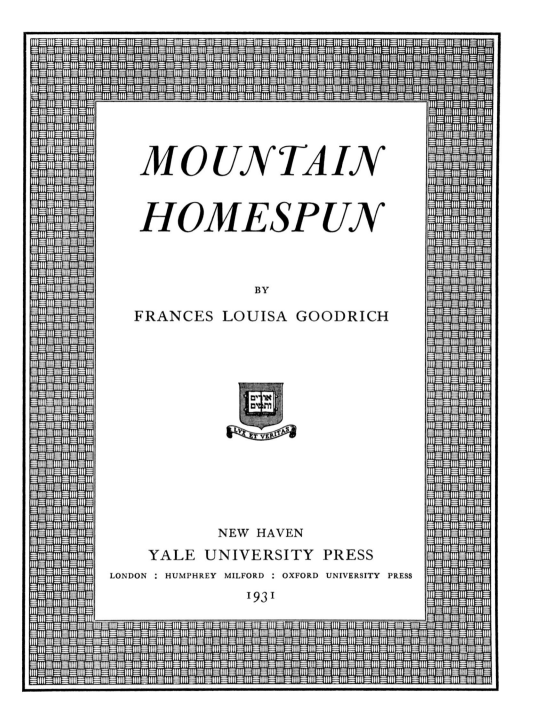

NEW HAVEN

YALE UNIVERSITY PRESS

LONDON : HUMPHREY MILFORD : OXFORD UNIVERSITY PRESS

1931

THE AMASA STONE MATHER
MEMORIAL PUBLICATION FUND

The present volume is the fourteenth work published by the Yale University Press on the Amasa Stone Mather Memorial Publication Fund. This Foundation was established August 25, 1922, by a gift to Yale University from Samuel Mather, Esq., of Cleveland, Ohio, in pursuance of a pledge made in June, 1922, on the fifteenth anniversary of the graduation of his son, Amasa Stone Mather, who was born in Cleveland on August 20, 1884, and was graduated from Yale College in the Class of 1907. Subsequently, after traveling abroad, he returned to Cleveland, where he soon won a recognized position in the business life of the city and where he actively interested himself also in the work of many organizations devoted to the betterment of the community and to the welfare of the nation. His death from pneumonia on February 9, 1920, was undoubtedly hastened by his characteristic unwillingness ever to spare himself, even when ill, in the discharge of his duties or in his efforts to protect and further the interests committed to his care by his associates.

This book is dedicated to

JULIA WEBSTER GOODRICH

and to the memory of

EDITH FISH SHELTON

ACKNOWLEDGMENT

THIS *is the record of a generation that is gone. The homespun world of which it tells is vanished. You will not find Lonesome Creek though you hunt for it. A few of us, to whom it was dear, hold it still in our hearts, and to us it is living.*

So many people have helped with this book that I cannot name them all. There is the one who first proposed my writing down what had been gathered in thirty-five years; there are those who have criticized and suggested in a way that helped; and more than to all others a debt is owed to the people of the Southern Mountains, who taught me much and who called me friend.

Two of these must be named: the wise-hearted women, Elmeda McHargue Walker, master weaver of coverlets, and Susie Dudley Shelton, weaver and artist.

F. L. G.

Asheville, North Carolina,
June, 1930.

CONTENTS

PART I. THE CRAFTS

PART II. THE PEOPLE

APPENDIXES

Illustrations

PART I. THE CRAFTS

Them hath he filled with wisdom of heart, to work all manner of work, of the engraver, and of the cunning workman, and of the embroiderer, in blue, and in purple, in scarlet and in fine linen, and of the weaver, even of them that do any work, and of those who devise cunning work.

EXODUS

1. THE OLD CRAFTS

WEAVING

IN the grounds of Mount Vernon, hard by the flower beds of Martha Washington, there is a small building filled with implements strange to the eyes of many of this generation, but of the first utility in old times. There are spinning wheels large and small, foot-power looms, heckles, flax brakes, reels, winding blades, and many other objects—all for one end, the home manufacture of fabrics. In the museum at Deerfield, Massachusetts, in that of Doylestown, Pennsylvania, and in other museums, one finds similar equipment preserved.

These exhibits testify to the knowledge of weaving brought from the various communities and countries on the other side of the sea whence the bands of colonists came to this new land. To one who has learned their use, these well-worn tools are of special interest and seem to bring near the sturdy, faith-keeping men and women who used them and who fought the battle of the wilderness for us.

These exhibits are not all that is left to tell the story of the old crafts, for throughout the eastern states of our country may be found specimens of the work done on the looms.

In New England the practice of home weaving was in general abandoned long ago, though lingering, doubtless, in remote spots until after the 1850's. There are many old coverlets in good preservation, some woven in the more common fashion with overshot designs, on four sets of "harness," others on six sets; more rarely one is found woven on five sets, and a few beautiful specimens remain of the true "double weave," which required eight or more sets of harness. There are homespun blankets, too, and linen sheets and table linen; bits of linen from dresses, one with a crossbar of copperas, yellow on pure white, and preserved as the lining of a quilt.

In one farmhouse in New Hampshire is kept what was known as a "frock," a man's garment, smocklike in shape and very long. It is woven of blue wool on a cotton warp in a fine, close pattern. This was worn by a farmer in his winter drives to the village, the long skirts tucked about his feet, up to the year 1880.

From New York and from Pennsylvania come many fine coverlets, and other states are not behind. To testify to this home industry in Virginia, we have the word of Thomas Jefferson, who wrote to John Adams on January 21, 1812:

Every family in the country is a manufactory within itself and is very generally able to make within itself all the stout and middling stuffs for its own clothing and household use. We consider a sheep for every person in the family as sufficient to clothe it, in addition to the cotton, hemp and flax which we raise ourselves. We use little machinery. The spinning jenny and loom with the flying shuttle can be managed in a family; but nothing more complicated. The economy and thriftiness resulting from our household manufactures are such that *they will never again be laid aside;* and nothing more salutary for us has ever happened than the British obstructions to our demands for their manufactures. Restore free intercourse when they will, their commerce with us will have totally changed its form, and the articles we shall in future want from them will not exceed their own consumption of our produce.

It takes nothing from the interest of these words that the households of the United States no longer depend on the output of their home looms to supply their needs.

In the fastnesses of the southern Appalachian Mountains the change came much later than in other parts of the country. Forty years ago there was a wealth of homespun fabrics to be found, and in communities remote from towns the very work of preparing thread and of weaving cloth was going on in much the same fashion as of old, with no thought of a market outside the neighborhood. A skilful weaver of coverlets took the wool as it came from the backs of sheep belonging to a well-to-do neighbor and worked it up "on shares," thus getting her own supply of linsey or blanket or coverlet, without exchange of money. Many a woman in the mountains was weaving linsey for the petticoats of her womankind and jeans for the men-folk. If the work was paid in money, the prices were fixed: for carding and spinning wool, three pounds to the dollar. Plain weaving was paid at the rate of eight yards to the dollar, and the weaving of a coverlet brought a dollar for every four yards.

In a truly homespun family of those days and for long after, the sheets, the towels, the blankets, the coverlets, and the counterpanes had been made in the house and were replenished as needed. Often the store of coverlets filled a shelf in the best room from floor to ceiling, ready to be added to the marriage portion of the daughters. A sojourner in the mountains in 1890 had the chance, if so minded, to learn the secrets of this craft.

Of all the fabrics, the coverlets were the most interesting. They were of lighter weight than those in the North, as befitted the milder climate, and were almost all in overshot designs. In very old ones the cotton was hand

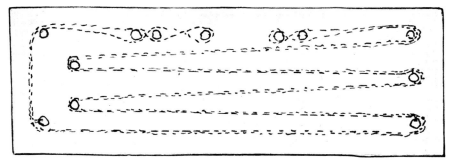

Arrangement of Warping Bars, showing how "chain" is placed
around the pegs.

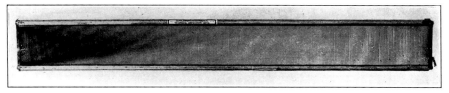

The Sley or Reed.

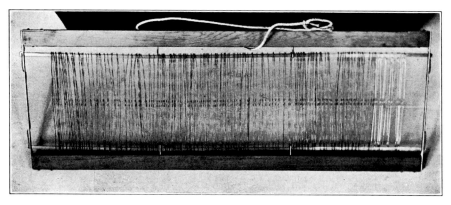

Harness Set or Heddle Frame.

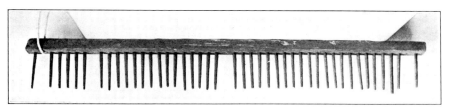

The Rake.

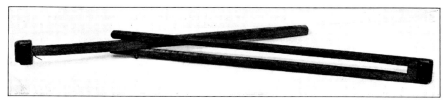

The Temples, used to keep the web stretched while weaving.

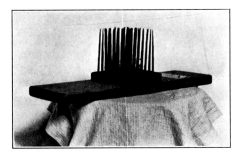

The Heckle.

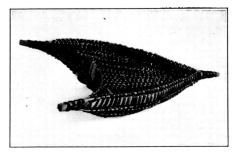

Picking Basket.

The Scotching Knife.

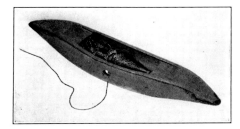

Shuttle with Quill holding yarn.

Flax Brake.

Winding Blades.

spun. Later, cotton thread was bought from small country mills under the name of "bunch thread."

The wool was prepared entirely by hand, being first washed, then picked over to rid it of burrs and other "trash." If the dyeing was done "in the wool," which insured a more even color but made the wool harder to work, this was the time for it. Next came the carding, a wearisome job, hard on the shoulders. It was done with wool cards—two flat pieces of wood, ten inches long by four inches broad, each with a handle, and with one side of each card set with short, bent, wire teeth to comb the wool. These cards are still in the market. There are also cotton cards and mixing cards, these to break up the matted wool and to mix the colors if more than one is to be spun together to make yarn. With the wool cards the wool was combed and fashioned into a long, thin roll, ready for the spinner. Before being carded the wool was well greased with lard; and if the coloring was done after spinning, the yarn was washed with care or the dye would not take.

The large wool wheel is familiar by sight to most of us, though we may not have heard its rhythmic whir nor have seen the fine attitudes into which the spinner is thrown by the action. The southern wheels are smaller in diameter and are set higher than those in New England.

To form a center to her "broach" or spindleful of yarn, the spinner winds a corn shuck about her spindle, takes the end of a roll in her left hand and with her right hand on the wheel begins her task, a task so graceful that it looks easy. When the spindle is full, the broach is slipped off and laid aside till the day's stint is done. Then the yarn is wound off onto the reel and tied up into skeins, usually of a half pound. A skein was often in old times spoken of as a "yard," because it was supposed to fill a yard of cloth.

The cotton for the coverlet warp and for part of the filling was "spooled," being wound from the skeins placed on the "winding blades" to spools made of corncobs, burnt through with a hot iron, or onto regular yarn spools, if one possessed them.

The warping of the cotton thread—that is, putting it into shape to be transferred as warp to the back beam of the loom—is an essential process but hard to describe. The warping bars are a series of wooden pegs, seven or eight inches long, driven in a certain order into the end of a barn or into a wooden frame that can be set in a convenient place. There must be a clear space in front of it for the spool frame and for the stepping to and fro of the warper. In the spool frame are the spools filled with thread, held in place by willow wands. The warper first calculates how many "bouts" it will take to fill out her web, whether it be narrow or wide, and then gathering a number of the threads in her hand she carries them to the bars and lays them under and over the pegs until she has completed a circuit—the "bout." At the end of each bout she "picks the cross," dividing the threads on her fingers and laying half of them on one side of certain pegs and half on the other side. When all the bouts are completed, she ties the "crosses" —the crossed threads—in such a way as to keep them apart at that point, and then takes the warp from the bars, looping it onto itself to make a chain of heavy, soft, white links, and the onlooker understands why the warp is called, in the mountains, the "chain."

For the "beaming" and "drawing through," a whole day's work is required; that is, for rolling the chain evenly onto the back or warp beam of the loom, passing it through the "rake" on the way, to divide it properly, and drawing each separate thread through the harness eye indicated for it in the "draft" or pattern and through the slits in the reed or "sley." The process requires more than one pair of hands, but after the chain is safely and smoothly on the beam a very young child can sit on the weaver's bench in front and take the ends of the threads as they are passed through the harness. Many a mountain-born man and woman has now a vivid recollection of wearisome hours thus spent as "a little fellow," and with the abandonment of looms as useless plunder this irksome task is all that has ever been known to some of them of the art of hand weaving.

In far-back times, "enduring of the war," when all the men-folk were away and the women were straining every nerve to keep the souls and bodies of their households together, the "little-uns" had still another part to play as they held flaming pine torches "way up into the night" so that the mother could see to weave on at "twelve yards to the dollar."

When the yarn for the woof or "filling," both wool and cotton, was wound onto the quills that fit into the shuttles, and when the "gears" were adjusted so that the harness sets moved with due precision, the work of weaving a coverlet could begin and the weaver had at last the pleasure of seeing the result of all the toil of preparation. One of the best weavers in North Carolina, producing coverlets in her eightieth year, said she would choose nothing different than to weave on, were she to live her life over again. "It is so pretty to see the flowers come out," for it is as flowers that the design shows itself to the happy thrower of the shuttle.

HOW THE LOOM GREW

Weaving, in the terms of a good definition, is the process by which threads of any substance are interlaced so as to form a continuous web.

It is an industry or art so ancient that its origin is not known. Alfred Barlow in his *History of Weaving* speaks of the oldest specimen of weaving so far discovered: "A kind of cloth which appears to be flax," found in the ancient Swiss lake dwellings, supposed to have belonged to the Stone Age.

The simplest form of weaving consists of one set of long fibers, natural or twisted into a continuous thread by spinning, laid side by side—the warp, across which another set of fibers, the woof or filling, lies interlaced at right angles, the woof threads being passed under and over the warp threads alternately, so making a web.

The earliest weavers doubtless used material ready to their hand. To quote Barlow again:

> In Loanga the weavers make their cloth to this day of a grass two feet high, which grows untilled in the desert plains and needs no preparation to be put to work. The length of the grass is the length of the web and they make the cloth rather narrower than long. This cloth is woven like ours; but they make it on their knees without shuttle or loom, having the patience to pass the woof through the web with their fingers.

From this grass cloth, woven without aid to the hand of man, to the most intricately woven product of a Jacquard loom today, the principle of weaving remains the same. This is more apparent in what is known as plain weaving than in pattern weaving. Plain weaving looks like the ordinary linen used for dresses. It may be illustrated by the well-known process of ordinary darning, in which the cross threads go alternately under and over the longitudinal threads. In weaving on a loom the longitudinal threads are called the warp or chain, and the cross threads the woof or filling. The method of weaving plain cloth, however differing in material and in fineness of thread, has changed merely in substituting for the fingers various implements.

It was a great day for the craft when the first thread was spun, twisting short fibers together into a continuous thread of indefinite length, and the web therefore lengthened. But with a longer web and softer thread there arose the need of some contrivance to hold the warp threads in place, stretched out at an even tension. This had to be done in such a way that the threads could be held taut or loosened at will. A simple way to accomplish this, still in use in some parts of the world, is to fasten one end of the warp to the trunk of a tree. The weaver, sitting on the ground at the requisite distance, passes a cord from the other end of the warp around his body, and by leaning forward or back, loosens or tightens the web as he desires.

Here we have the origin of the idea of the two beams in a modern hand loom, the tree trunk corresponding to the back beam on which the warp is first wound, and the man's body to the cloth beam, to which are attached the forward ends of the warp and on which the web of cloth is rolled as the work proceeds.

At first, even in the longer webs made possible by the invention of spinning, the passing of the woof threads over and under the threads of the warp was done with the fingers. The Berber women of northern Africa still work without a shuttle, passing the ball of yarn for the filling of their *burnouses* in and out by hand. Long ago, however, some genius discovered a way to separate the threads of the warp, raising every other one and so making a passage, called the "shed," for the woof thread which, carried in a smooth shuttle, could then be shot from one side of the web to the other through the shed. For passing the thread back across the web, however, the warp threads that were raised had to be lowered, and the alternate threads raised; when this problem was solved, the art of weaving was well on its way.

From very simple methods for opening the sheds for the shuttle's passage there developed in the course of time the "gears" and "harness" of the now old-fashioned hand looms with which we are concerned. Another contrivance was in very early times found useful and even necessary—something to push or beat up each thread or filling as it was put in, pressing it against the thread in front of it and so making firm the cloth. In the so-called Colonial loom the sley or reed, swung in the batten, takes its place. It is worth noting here that all the machinery or contrivances in the hand loom of which we speak, between the back beam and the breast and cloth beams, which to the uninitiated have so mysterious an aspect, are there to accomplish these two purposes: to open the sheds for the shuttle and to comb the woof threads firmly into place. If this is borne in mind the description of the process of weaving will be more readily understood.

Since the days of the type of hand loom commonly used in the southern mountains, many contrivances have been added to foot-power looms, and various methods have been invented to make easier the labor of the hand weaver. But we are concerned here not with these, but with the older ways of the mountain weavers.

COVERLET DRAFTS

In the "drawing in" and in the actual weaving of a coverlet, a design or pattern is necessary and this was called a draft. The good offices of a preacher

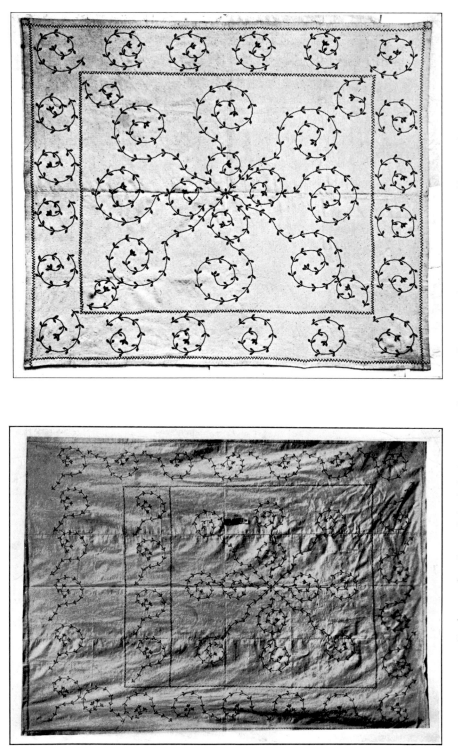

Bedspreads with original design worked on hand-woven cloth by Susie Dudley Shelton.

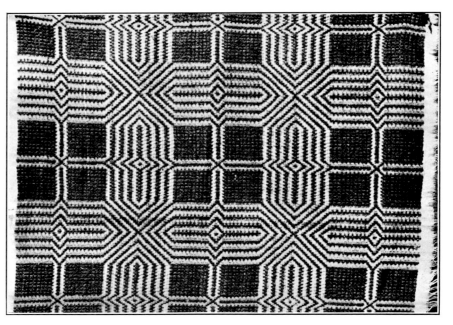

Coverlet Pattern: "The Flower of May."

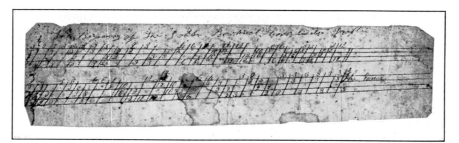

The Draft for the Brown and White "Double Bowknot" Coverlet,
by which it was woven.

Draft for "The Flower of May" Coverlet, with dashes in
place of figures.

or lawyer were often called upon to "draw off," that is, to copy, a draft. It was written on a narrow slip of paper, from four inches to half a yard long according to the length of one unit of the pattern and was fastened on the front of the loom in plain sight of the weaver. Old drafts are often written on the backs of letters or bills or law papers. The draft consists of lines and figures, or—if the weaver could not read figures—of lines only, mystifying to the uninitiated. These may be found in many an old house tucked away in trunks and cupboards, rolled up and tied carefully with thread. When spread out they are seen to be marked with multitudinous pin pricks as one worker and another has put in a pin to keep her place in the "drawing in."

The names of the patterns are a study in themselves, and fall naturally into groups. There are the drafts in which there is a real or fancied resemblance to natural objects, such as "Beautiful Wave," "The Rising and the Setting of the Sun," "Flowers of May," "Lilies of the Valley and of the Meadows." "Flowers of Edinboro" must have come from the old country, and "Dogwood Blossoms" and "Rattlesnake" tell of their origin or their renaming in this new land.

Two at least of the drafts bear dates: "Crosseawise" from Ireland, 1769, and "Germany's Star," 1754. "St. Ann's Robe" must have been brought from Ireland and so must the "Irish Chain" and "Double Irish Chain." Some patterns are now called by different names in different localities, and new patterns have been made by recombining motifs or by changing proportions. In this latter way "St. Ann's Robe" seems to have become "Governor's Garden" and then "Beauty of Kaintuck." Next it appears as "Polk and Dallas" (written on the draft "Pokendalis"). Its last change of name is to "Rocky Mountain Cucumber."

In like ways "Braddock's Defeat," in which one can almost see the ranks of British regulars, appears again in a slightly different form as "President's View," and "Boney Parte's March" is very similar to these.

Why "Downfall of Paris" should be like "Sunrise on the Walls of Troy" is hard to tell. What is the date of the "Fair Walls of Coventry"? "Federal City" reminds us that the city of Washington was so called in common speech for many years. We find "Indian War," "The Thirteen Original States," "Jaffison's Buty," "Mt. Vernon," and "White House" dating themselves, as well as "Washington's Diment Ring." "Whig Rose," drawn through the harness as usual but woven by using another draft in the "tramping" or treadling, turns into "Texas Beauty," and with another change by a skilled weaver, fifteen years ago, it became "Elmeda's Fancy." "Water Waves" is identical with "Double Bow Knot" and with "Muscadine Hulls." There are countless Wheel drafts such as "Iron Wheel," the "Wheel of Fortune," "Chariot Wheel," and so on. The reverse side of "Rattlesnake," mentioned above, has a name to itself, "Cat Track and Snail Trail."

COUNTERPANES

THE "Countypin" drafts, for weaving white cotton counterpanes, are rather different from the drafts for the coverlets. Few women understood them, for they call for quite a different system of "tramping" of treadles. The names are less picturesque though "Huckabuck and Satan Stripe" is at first view alarming. Substitute "i" in the last part of Satan and the name is more befitting a bedspread.

THE WORKING OF FLAX

IN the old times much flax was raised and worked in the mountains and there are still a few specimens of coverlet weaving where linen was used with the wool in place of cotton, showing how all coverlets were made before cotton was obtainable.

The raising and working of flax was a long process and an arduous one. First it must be sown on Good Friday, five seeds in a space that can be covered by a man's thumb. In August it was pulled and bound into bundles; later, preferably in February, it was spread out in the fields to ret. The work with the flax brake came next and this, which broke the coarse, outer fiber of the stalk, was a man's job. So was the scotching done with a broad, blunt scotching knife of wood. Seeing the scotching of flax, which bruises the fiber but does not destroy it, one understands the proverb about the snake that was scotched, but not killed.

The heckling, or drawing the flax over the sharp teeth of the heckle, was hard work, but it was often done by women. After this the flax was ready to be put on the distaff (often called the rock in the southern mountains, as in Scotland), to be spun on the little flax wheel. The tow, or refuse from the scotching, and the better tow left after the heckling, was also spun for making coarse sheets or bedticking and for shirts for little boys, who found it very scratchy until several washings had rid it of the sticks.

COTTON

IN the early days cotton was raised in small patches in the more open parts of the mountains, or brought from the lowlands. This was spun by hand either on the flax wheel or on the big wool wheel. When small mills were established here and there it was cheaper, counting the labor required for the hand spinning, to buy the cotton thread from the mill. There are not many fast dyes for cotton to be found in the fields and woods, but copperas was cheap and effective either raw or burnt, and it did not injure the fiber of the cotton. Indigo and madder were used, and turkey red and the ever useful butternut. With a few other dyes, such as maple bark and hickory, a good variety of tints was obtained for the "cotton checks" and striped cotton homespuns for shirts and dresses. The arranging of stripes and colors gave room for the exercise of taste and for a pleasant rivalry among weavers. For a Sunday dress in summer an all white cotton fabric was most highly prized.

LINSEY-WOOLSEY

In winter no one need be cold, for there was linsey-woolsey (contracted now to linsey) originally woven, as its full name implies, of woolen thread on a linen warp. Long ago cotton was substituted for the linen. The weaving of this was what is called plain weaving, drawn in without need of a pattern, on two sets of harness and tramped with two treadles. If striped, the striping ran across the web, as the colors could readily be changed in the shuttles at the will of the weaver, while the chain must remain of one color throughout the web. In a plain but bright color the linsey was often made up into winter shirts or jerkins for the men, and either plain or striped it furnished petticoats and dresses for the women and girls.

Though I do not vouch for the following story, telling of the old-time fabrics, it bears the marks of truth:

The fabric of which the vest was made was the glory and the climax of the old Kentucky hand-loom. It was a linsey-woolsey affair with gorgeous stripes running horizontal on the front waist, the colors, red, blue, green, yellow, white and so on. One Sunday in early autumn, more than sixty years ago, in a village in —— County, the preacher, dressed in a handsome new suit of grey-mixed jeans wore also a vest of linsey-woolsey that was a dream of elegance and beauty. He was a comely young man and his was an eloquent tongue. In the congregation was a pious old sister, beloved of all, as Aunt Betsy Axewell. She was noted for the beauty of the fabrics her loom turned out and especially lovely was her linsey-woolsey. A sincere and pious Christian, she was emotional and just simply bound to shout during the singing of the hymn after the sermon. On this occasion she was greatly wrought up and in the midst of her rhapsody she charged her bosom friend and crony thus: "Deep blue, pale blue, turkey red and white—Good gracious Maria, don't forget that stripe." She was taking the pattern of the preacher's vest, which she was firmly resolved to duplicate.

JEANS

THE jeans suits of which we hear so much in stories were also woven on a warp of cotton, but required at least three sets of harness to give the twill to the cloth. Mixed yarn of black and white or blue and white was a favorite for the woof of jeans, and the wool of a black sheep was also much used.

WARPS AND SLEYS

IN weaving coverlets, counterpanes, linsey, cotton dresses, and jeans, the warp was "full-sleyed," that is, two threads were put through each slit of the sley or reed, making the cloth firm and solid. For weaving blankets the warp threads were often "thirded," as it was called, which is to say that two were put in one slit, one in the next, and so on, alternating two threads and one thread across the web. This made a softer fabric and allowed the woof to be beaten up more closely covering the warp and making a warmer blanket. For a "single-sleyed" web one thread only is put in each slit, with a heavy warp thread. This answers well for the weaving of a rag rug.

"Flatting" the warp thread—that is, so drawing the threads through the harness eyes that the threads of the warp are raised and depressed in sets or pairs of two instead of singly as in plain weaving—was also used in the weaving of blankets or in any cloth where a basket effect was desired.

Rarely did a mountain weaver use a warp of wool. Now and then one finds an old shawl thus woven, but for most uses the cotton chain was deemed suitable.

LOOMS

THE looms were of the so-called Colonial type, large and heavy. There was a saying current, "The heavier the loom the lighter for the weaver." It must have been a man who said it first. The looms were of two general kinds: in one, the batten swung from the framework above and the loom therefore took much headroom. The other, the "little rocking loom," had a batten rocking back and forth on pins in the lower side bars.

It was not always easy to get room and a good light on the web for one of these looms in a mountain home, and a place for it was sometimes made on the wide porch, or under a slight roofing at one end of the house. Those who followed weaving as a livelihood, or were more than ordinarily interested in the craft, made room inside the house, that cold weather might not stop the work, or built them a little loom house in the yard with chimney and fireplace. Here could be kept all the appurtenances and on the walls could be hung the hanks of varicolored yarn ready to the hand.

DYEING

IT may have been in the 1870's or 1880's that the Diamond Dyes began to creep in to replace the old vegetable coloring. They caught the eye of the dwellers among drab surroundings, and seemed, as one of them said, "brighter and more beautifuller" than the old dyes, which were discarded in many localities. It was easier, too, to buy a packet at the crossroads store than to search the woods for material. It is true that indigo was a "boughten dye," but its quality had deteriorated and the conduct of a blue pot, always a ticklish business, was becoming more and more uncertain.

Looking at the rule below one readily sees that for success in the indigo dyeing both experience and judgment were necessary. The conditions under which it was carried on were not those of a chemical laboratory and did not permit a hard and fast recipe. Much was guesswork. Many factors entered in, such as the strength of the madder and indigo, and above all of the home-dripped lye; the temperature at which the pot was kept varying even in the chimney corner as the fire on the hearth was built up or allowed to die down. The process is one of fermentation. When it has reached the right stage and the liquid will color a fast dye, it is said to have "come." The sign of its "coming" or being "about to come" is its turning green and foamy.

Few women became adepts, but those few produced unvaryingly a fine, clear blue. A large iron pot, holding a number of gallons, is the first requisite in the process. It is well if the pot has been used before for blue, for it takes a great deal of indigo to color a pot before it begins to dye the wool. Here is an old recipe for a blue pot:

½ bushel pot full of warm water,
2 ounces of indigo in a little sack,
2 ounces of madder, or as much as you rub through of indigo.
1 teacup of wheat bran, or two handfuls,
½ pint of drip lye, or enough to make the bran feel slick or till water has a sweet taste.

Soak the indigo in the sack till soft, say twelve hours, then rub part through into the warm water, leave sack in water, add as much madder as the indigo rubbed out, add the bran and the lye. Keep the pot warm till the dye "comes," it may take a few days or two weeks. It is quicker if you have some "yeast," (that is, the lees of a former blue pot) to add to this pot. It will foam and turn green when ready.

Some say "let the pot set," keeping it warm till it "comes," without stirring. Others say "dip it up each day with a cup," others say "once an hour," but all agree that it must be so dipped after the pot "comes." One dye mixer says that the first indication of this is "not the looks but the smell"; and well it may be. One who has been in the room where the blue pot sits cozily by the open fireplace is not likely to forget the smell; but though fearful, it is entirely innocuous.

To go on with the recipe:

Try the yarn. If too pale the lye may be too strong or too weak. If too strong, the bran will feel very slick. (Others say it will feel rough and almost burn the hand.) After dipping hang the wool or yarn in the air (to oxidize it), then dip again and so on. Some let the wool lie in the dyepot over night, others one hour. For pale blue, "dip till color is right"—about five times; for deep blue, many times more. After dipping a lot of blue, "renew up" the pot by rubbing out more indigo and adding madder, bran and lye. Lay a plate over the bran to keep it down while the wool is in.

When the right depth of color is obtained, wash the wool in warm water to get out the lye which would otherwise rot the wool. If cotton or flax is to be colored it must be done before any wool goes into the pot. When blue is wholly exhausted, add indigo, bran, madder and lye and let stand over night or till it "comes."

Another favorite dye for coverlets was madder. This also could be bought, but if raised in the garden and used fresh it was much brighter, as the roots soon lose strength after digging. Coloring with madder is a much easier process than blue dyeing, and requires less time for fermentation.

This is one rule for coloring wool with madder:

1 bushel of bran. Add warm water till thinner than bread. Let it stand and sour. (If weather is warm, one day and a night will be enough.) Pour it into a sack and let the water drip off. If not enough water to cover yarn, add more to the bran and let it drip through. 1 teacup of madder to each "yard" of yarn, or 1 pound of madder to each 3 pounds of yarn. Add to water, put in yarn and boil till right color, 2 or 3 hours. If not to suit, dip in weak suds or lye. This will turn it redder. Rinse in clear water to get out the lye.

According to another rule the yarn is soaked in alum water overnight before coloring and the bran is not soured unless yarn is desired deep in color. There is also a recipe for coloring cotton and flax with madder, with this note: "If wool is dyed by this rule it turns yellow brown and then if boiled in soapsuds it turns pink." When raised in the garden it was kept "hilled up" and at any time a quantity of the fine roots could be dug up, dried, and beaten up for use. Wild madder was used occasionally but was not very effective. It answered well for the blue pot when home-grown or "boughten" madder was not available.

Aunt Judy's rule for coloring wool a beautiful, rich black is as follows: "Put some walnut roots in a big pot with a good deal of water; fling in some sumac berries or sourwood leaves; put in the wool or yarn and bile it rale good. Then turn the pot upside down on the ground and leave it there all night. This sets the dye."

There are many dye plants giving browns in various hues. Alder tags (catkins), chestnut-oak bark, spruce-pine bark, black walnut bark and hulls and leaves all yield browns.

The process of coloring was almost always carried on out of doors in a big iron pot under which the fire was made. One of the most valued dye plants was called "bay leaves" (botanically, *Symplocos tinctoria*), which grows only in certain localities. The leaves contain a bright and fast yellow dye for wool; they should be gathered when mature, but before frost touches them. Wash the wool thoroughly before dyeing yellow; lay the leaves and yarn in the pot alternately, cover with water, and boil half a day. Some dip the yarn in weak lye after this and rinse in fair water thoroughly.

Another reliable plant is a species of coreopsis that is found on rocky ridges at the height of four thousand feet above sea level. The flowers are gathered as soon as they bloom in August, and a handful is thrown into the pot on each layer of yarn. The color produced is an orange, very rich. If used after dyeing with "bay leaves," it turns the wool orange red, a very fine color. It will be there as long as there is a thread of the cloth left, but moths are said to be particularly fond of wool colored with "dye flowers," as coreopsis is called in the mountains.

There are many other dye plants that produce yellow. To make a true green, one of these was used first and then the yarn was dipped in the indigo pot to turn it green. Any yellow dye would do, but hickory bark or black-oak bark or broom sedge was preferred unless a very bright green was needed, when peach tree leaves were chosen for the yellow. An olive green could be obtained without the aid of the blue pot by using hickory or red-oak bark and copperas. "Boil bark till dark as you think it ought to be. Put in copperas and yarn. Boil until yarn is dark enough."

Sassafras seems to be a most useful plant. Its flowers will dye wool a bright yellow, the bark colors red-brown, and the root in combination with plum bark makes a red-brown of a different hue. Broom sedge is said to make a different hue for each month of the year but it is most effective when cut green. The yellow sneezeweed yields a good yellow, but it is not fast color.

There are fewer good home dyes for cotton, but for the coverlets the cotton was rarely colored, being used in its own creamy white. For the scarlet wool in a coverlet made in the eighties was used what the weaver called "Scotch chenille" (cochineal?).

NEEDLEWORK

ALONG with the work of the wheel and loom went that of the needle. Sometimes these were combined, as in the making of window curtains of white cotton, loosely woven, with a border of drawn work, but the threads were left out in the weaving instead of being pulled out from the finished cloth, and the needlework was done while the web was still a-weaving.

SPREADS TUFTED AND KNOTTED

THERE are many good specimens of old tufted and knotted spreads. The earliest are made of homespun cloth, the designs often original. "Grandma Duncan," in North Carolina, brought in flowers from her dooryard, cockscombs and marigolds and many more, and wrought their shapes into the spread that is treasured by her great-grandchildren.

QUILTS

QUILTS have been made since time immemorial. Naturally most of these were "scrap quilts," for thrift called for the using of odd bits of material on hand, but every woman longed to make at least one quilt, either "pieced" or of "patchwork," that is, of *appliqué* work, out of new cloth with colors of her own choosing. Each pattern had a name and these ranged from "Tree of Paradise" to "Eight Ways of Contrariness."

One "powerful working woman," who was also an artist in her work, embroidered home-woven sheets for bedspreads in designs of her own invention. She used a chain stitch and with homespun thread colored with indigo and with turkey red she produced charming results.

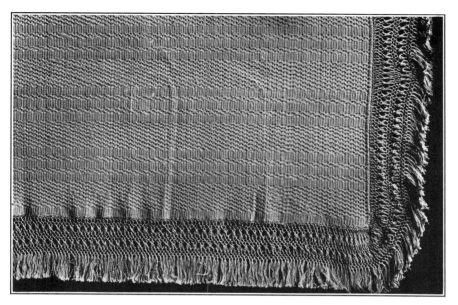

"County Pin": Honeycomb Pattern.

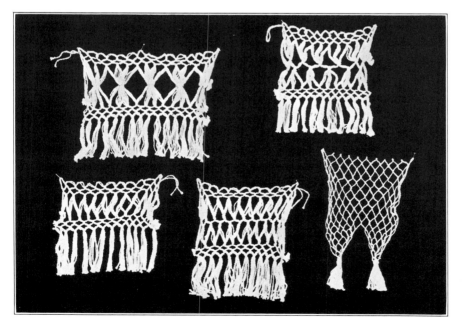

Handmade Fringes

Patchwork Quilt (*appliqué*), "Rose Wreath"—An old pattern.

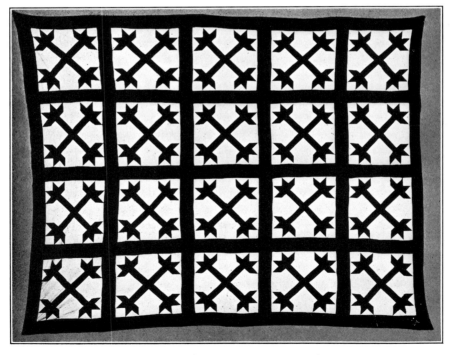

Pieced Quilt, "Texas Cross Roads."

Fringes were made in various patterns, of wool or more commonly of cotton thread, for the edges of the coverlets, counterpanes, and spreads and for testers as well.

The making of hooked rugs was also followed, though it was not so common a craft as weaving or needlework.

BASKETS

THE craft of basket making would seem to have been brought from the old countries by settlers in the southern mountains. The change to the New World made possible and even necessary changes in materials, and in this respect something may have been learned from the Indians. For large or strong baskets osiers were exchanged for splits of white oak or of hickory wood. Much work and much skill goes into the making of a split basket. First the tree must be chosen not over one foot in diameter at the butt, of straight growth, and of firm fiber. Even best judges are sometimes mistaken in a tree, finding it twisted or of loose growth, and are obliged to abandon it after felling. When the trunk has been sawed or chopped into convenient lengths, these are split into halves and again into quarters and eighths, from which the ribs and hoops and "weavers" can be rived off. In this way every split that is used in the basket is worked out with the grain of the wood, instead of being cut across the fibers as in machine-made baskets, and in this the durability and beauty of the handmade basket largely consists. There is much to do with the knife and the drawknife, shaving and shaping, before the hoops and ribs and smaller splits are ready. The care taken in this is one of the chief factors in a perfect basket.

The most common shape is what is known as the melon basket or hip basket. It is interesting to note that this shape is to be seen in pictures in the *National Geographic Magazine,* from Ireland, Roumania, and Jamaica, and has been found throughout central and southern Europe. Perhaps the idea is a very ancient one, and therefore is widespread.

The starting point of these and like shapes is made with two hoops firmly fastened together at right angles to each other. One of these forms the rim or edge of the basket; half of the other hoop forms the handle, and the rest, passing under the basket, makes a strong support for the whole structure. The handle may be depended upon to hold as long as there is any basket left. The hoops may be round, or one or both may be oval to make an oval-shaped basket, or to give an extra long handle, or they may be bent to give a square edge or squared handle. There would seem to have been only a few shapes in use in the old days, but those now used are all variants of the one idea, and are a natural development.

On another plan, but still of the dependable splits, were fashioned hampers for the storing and carrying of grain, and there were long, open baskets for the rolls of the spinners.

There was much diversity in the workmanship. A good craftsman made a melon basket that would securely hold wheat or other grain for sowing. Some were so skilful that even clover seed could not sift through. Prices were fixed according to size, as a one-peck, two-peck, or half-bushel basket, and so on. In barter it was the custom to allow the basket maker as much corn as the basket would hold.

It was natural that some use should be made of willow, for osiers are the chief basket material of Europe. In this country it was wrought only into light baskets, for sewing, for carrying eggs and other light stuff to market. A favorite shape was the form of a cup and a saucer woven together, but this was chiefly for ornament.

A material less common is the bulrush, bound with a thin oak split. These rush baskets were made by the Indians as well as by white settlers, and were frequently in the shape of a squat jar, with a cover, very large and useful for storing "household plunder." The Indians made use also of river cane for basketry.

CHAIRS AND BROOMS AND TUBS AND SO FORTH

White oak splits were the usual material used for seating homemade chairs. The frames were worked out of hickory or maple, or black walnut, without the aid of a lathe. For the seats some preferred to use twisted rushes or corn shucks.

Broom corn was grown on the farm and made into brooms by binding with the ever useful oak split. If the brooms gave out before the next crop was ready, the housewife gathered broom sedge and made a substitute. The hickory broom, made all in one piece, was almost indestructible and its work was effective on puncheon floors.

Good coopers seem to have been plentiful. Tubs, barrels, "stands" (that is, high tubs for holding salted meats and pickled beans and kraut) and piggins (for milking and similar uses) were abundant. The piggin, though unknown to many, is defined in Webster as "a small wooden pail or tub with upright stave as a handle." A very handy vessel it is.

It was almost a craft to "get out" the shingles and "boards" with which all buildings were covered. These were rived out with a froe from blocks of white pine or oak or chestnut. The heart of the wood yielded shingles that lasted a hundred years. Boards were longer than shingles and therefore made a rougher covering, suitable for sheds and barns.

For making shingles the log was sawed into eighteen-inch lengths and each block was split into wedge-shaped pieces from which the separate shingles were rived. They were supposed to average four inches in width. They were made of soft wood and shaved smooth with a drawknife, leaving them half an inch thick at one end and shaved to a thin edge at the other like the sawed shingle.

For the board, or clapboard as it is sometimes called, the log was sawed into two-foot lengths. The boards were made either of hard or of soft wood, as they were rarely smoothed, but were left rough and of the same thickness from end to end.

The rived-out shingle lasted a hundred years, since water ran off of it with little wear. This was its advantage over the modern shingle sawed across the grain.

The froe is unknown even in name to most people of these days. It consists of a dull blade of iron, some twelve inches long, fixed on a long handle. The blade is driven with a mallet into the section of tree trunk and the handle gives leverage to work it through the block, slitting as it goes.

POTTERY

Where the right sort of clay was to be found, a rough but attractive pottery was made in the shape of jugs and pitchers and wide-mouthed jars for holding dried fruit and pickles. The Cherokee and Soco Indians were adept in the potter's art and may have taught something of the craft to their new neighbors, but their work was unglazed while the mountain potter often obtained very good effects in green and gray glazes, although his aim was use rather than beauty.

The primitive potter used glass for glazing his pottery and some old potters in the mountains still use that method.

Any kind of glass, bottles or windowpanes, is collected, broken by pounding, until it will pass a certain sieve, and then ground to the required fineness between two revolving stones, like the old millstones, only much smaller.

This ground glass is mixed with wood ashes, iron ore, and clay in the proper proportions, is then wet with water to the right consistency, and is spread on the vessel to be glazed; after drying this is placed in the kiln where sufficient heat is maintained to melt the glass and to fuse it into the glaze.

This information came from an old potter in North Carolina, whose family have made pottery for eighty years and have used this method from the beginning. A modern potter from outside the mountains verified this in conversation as the method in use from old time by the mountain potters.

2. REVIVAL OF CRAFTS IN THE SOUTHERN APPALACHIANS

DURING the past thirty years a number of enterprises have been started for the preservation of the crafts of the southern Appalachian Mountains. Most of these ventures have been successful and are being carried on today. It may be of interest to tell in some detail of one of the earliest of these projects.

THE ALLANSTAND COTTAGE INDUSTRIES

THE Allanstand Cottage Industries grew out of pure neighborliness—on one side a gift, and on the other a desire to promote the happiness of the women of a mountain cove.

In the year 1895 two women were living together in Brittain's Cove, twelve miles from Asheville, North Carolina. In those days twelve miles was a long distance, and the journey to town, made in a mountain wagon or in the saddle, consumed three or four hours. Once in a while the men and older boys made the trip with tobacco and other produce; the children for some months of the year had school to keep their minds alert and happy; but for the women, life had less color; for them there were few or no outings, and many of them were shut in to monotony. One woman who had once been to the nearest railway station, five miles away, used to relate with excitement how "a freight and a passenger" had passed while she was there. Another, who lived well up under the Chestnut Knob, and rarely moved far from her own dooryard, specialized, for an interest in life, in herb teas for real or fancied complaints, and often had four of these going at once: "one for the head, one for the back, one for the chest and one for when you didn't feel very good."

One of the women in the cottage at the Cove taught the school; the other, finding a variety of occupations, was dubbed "the woman who runs things" at the cottage. While she was pondering the resources at hand for bringing healthful excitement into the lives of her neighbor women, one of them out of pure good will and affection brought to her as a gift a coverlet, forty years old, woven in the "Double Bowknot" pattern, golden brown on a cream-colored background. The brown had been dyed with chestnut oak, and was as fine a color as the day it was finished. With the coverlet was given the "draft" by which it was woven, a long strip of paper covered with figures very mysterious to the grateful recipient. The "woman who runs things" was "put to her studies." Here was a fine craft, dying out and desirable to revive. Did she hold the clue to her puzzle in her very hand?

Let her tell the rest in her own words:

In any attempts to revive the old crafts, two questions confronted us: could we produce the coverlets at a moderate cost? And if so, could we find or make a market for them? At that time there was in this country no general interest in such handicraft and little demand for handwoven fabrics.

The coverlet made a journey North and the admiration it received made me believe that if we in the Cove could produce the like, a market could be found. It was surely worth a trial, and in the trying we would at least have a good time. We were meeting one afternoon each week at the cottage for sewing and chatting and for a short religious service closing in time for all to get home for the evening milking and other chores. Few women could come to the Sunday School or preaching services after getting the children "fixed to go" and with the dinner to prepare, so that this midweek meeting was valued both socially and religiously. Consulting together we found that there was one loom in the Cove, stored away in a barn loft, and Aunt Jane knew how to weave "plain cloth." The loom was set up in our library with much talk of "harness" and "gears" and "sleys" and "rakes" and "temples."

"Do you know you are using obsolete words?" said a manufacturer of cloth from Rhode Island, when I spoke to him of the "sley."

We determined to begin by making a curtain of silk pieces after the manner of a rag rug. While we were busy in the meetings cutting and sewing the silk, of which a store had been sent us, one woman was dyeing the cotton "bunch thread" for the warp or chain. Using maple bark she produced a purple-gray, a good background for the shining silk of the "filling." "Now," said I, "we can go right to work with the loom." In spite of the politeness which forbade a smile, it was evident that I had said something very funny, and when it was explained that the thread must first be spooled and then warped on warping bars we all "took us a hearty laugh" together. No bars were at hand, nor experts to use them, but Mrs. G's Aunt Sallie over the mountain had bars and was an old hand at weaving. So one fine day an expedition started over the mountain. The thread, wound on to spools made of corncobs, was in a "flour-poke" fastened to the front of the saddle on Cherokee, our Indian pony. I rode, with Mrs. G's baby in my lap, and Mrs. G walked. Aunt Sallie was looking for us and first we must have dinner. Then we were taken to the end of the big barn where the pegs were driven in for "warping a chain." Aunt Sallie calculated the "bouts" and soon we were deep in the process of warping, even being allowed to lay the threads on the bar for one "bout" and to "pick the cross." Before nightfall we made a triumphal entry to the Cove with the chain in the sack, a new thing learned and the memory of a hearty welcome.

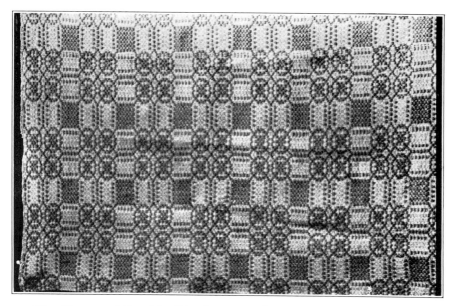

The Pattern "Double Chariot Wheel" which Elmeda Walker
wove for the Mountain Room in the White House.

The "Double Bowknot" Coverlet that started the Allanstand
Cottage Industries.

Salesroom of the Allanstand Cottage Industries.

Next we assisted (rather in the French fashion) in the beaming and drawing in of the warp and so learned a good deal more. Aunt Jane did the weaving and several yards of good silk tapestry rewarded our endeavors. This we felt was only a beginning, the making of coverlets being our goal. Wool was bought from a farmer near by, and Mrs. W's mother-in-law came over from the next cove to teach her how to set a "blue pot." It "came" well and part of our wool was dyed in it; part was colored with madder, a good red, and the rest was turned by boiling in walnut root "ooze" a rich, velvety black. When all was carded and spun we had enough yarn for three coverlets, two of the blue and one to be black and red.

Up on the Paint Fork of Ivy lived Squire Wesley Angel. His wife and daughters, "those Angel girls," so we were told, "could weave any kind of weaving." During the Christmas holidays the teacher and I rode over to Ivy, on Cherokee and a borrowed horse and so on up the Paint Fork. The distance was sixteen miles, the roads were bad, Ivy was "up" and we were slow and inexperienced riders, but we forded the river without disaster, avoided the deep mud holes in the road and reached our destination before dark came down upon us. We hallooed the house and when the Angels understood that we were friends of "Cousin Sallie W," they fairly pulled us from our steeds and made us at home. Their hearty kindness lives in our minds to this day.

Their home was one of the substantial, well-to-do dwellings where life in the mountains is at its best. They were truly a homespun family and the wealth of home-woven fabrics was amazing. When we got down to business, they would weave out our yarn. Mrs. Angel approved our undertaking. "If you haven't any get-up," she said, "you might as well have your box made."

What draft should we choose? I can still feel the bewilderment with which I surveyed the store of coverlets laid away carefully on shelves and brought out for our inspection. There was "Roan Mountain," "Big Works of Tennessee," "Cup and Saucer," "Winding Vine," "Missouri Trouble," and "Double Bowknot" and others. For the blue yarn we chose the "Double Bowknot," and the "Missouri Trouble" for the red and black. We learned that for every change of draft a day's work is required, so that in future it would be well to weave out each web in one pattern. We left our yarn and returned home the next day. Three weeks later, having sent a messenger to the Paint Fork, there was excitement at the cottage as we saw him returning with the web in a roll across the back of his saddle. There in one long strip were the three coverlets, so skilfully woven that, when cut out, the two lengths of each spread would join exactly in pattern.

The coverlets were easily sold, and while more yarn was preparing one of the women of our Cove undertook to learn the coverlet weaving from the Angels. Realizing that the market for large things like coverlets and curtains would be limited and that we must secure quick sales, we began to weave short lengths also, for table-runners, pillow tops, trunk covers and the like uses. Soon there were other looms going as the desire to learn this craft spread among us, and one was employed for weaving rugs in the coverlet patterns but with a heavier chain and by doubling and twisting the wool yarn. The weavers of plain cloths were engaged in making rag rugs or linsey, for coat suits, with wool filling on a cotton warp.

It was in 1897 that I went from Brittain's Cove to live at Allanstand, in Madison County. In the country about Allanstand hand-weaving was going on as in old times. In winter the men wore shirts of bright colored linsey and women and girls were clad in linsey dresses. Here much could be learned of dyes and of the working of wool and flax. By the time we realized that we had a real business on our hands, it was natural to give the industries the name of Allanstand and to make this place the center of the work.

Fortunately for the standard of our products a weaver of unusual skill and patience was one of the first to help us at Allanstand. It takes intelligence to be a thoroughly good coverlet weaver. Some women learn to do the work mechanically, but they never produce such good results as do those who have grasped the why and wherefore of it.

Elmeda Walker, who was born a McHargue, and who certainly had the spirit of her Scotch ancestors, did not live at Allanstand, but four miles away over the state line, in Tennessee. It was always a pleasure to go there. One rode by the short-cut through a hollow where rhododendrons met over the rider's head, then up a path a few inches wide to the top of the ridge and so along until one came to the tiny farm nestled in the fold of the hill, with the barn and the barn-lot and the house with its paled-in yard where beautiful things grew, March flowers, or Easters, red honeysuckle, flags, dahlias, all sorts of old-time flowers. But the best of it was the welcome of the three sisters of Highland blood who, like the three gray sisters, spun and wove and "slit the thin-spun thread." There was a hearty human sympathy here very unlike the ancient gray dames however, and an "old-time religion" of simple trust and love that was worth riding miles to find. The sisters had woven more webs than they could count, of coverlets and counterpanes and plain cloth; most of them being done on shares for their neighbors. Their market however had sadly dwindled as "store goods" came in fashion.

Their coverlets were woven "in the 800" which means, in modern parlance, on a reed, 20 to the inch, and so were fine and firm beyond any we had seen, for most weavers were content with using the 700 or even the 600 sley, making a much coarser cloth. Mrs. Walker's work hereafter set the standard for our Industries. To follow weaving was her delight and she followed it, producing for us beautiful webs, till she was long past eighty years of age.

When the Mountain Room in the White House was furnished by the first Mrs. Wilson, Mrs. Walker was chosen to weave the many yards of coverlet fabric for the furniture covering. We are loyal folk in the mountains and this task was the crowning experience of Elmeda Walker's life.

Hardly any other subject arouses so much enthusiasm and interest in a circle of mountain women as does the subject of weaving and its kindred arts. This is true whether the participants in the talk are themselves weavers or only their kinsfolk. Such work has for generations taken the place of all other artistic expression, and everyone, at least in the days of which I am telling, knew something by experience or by watching the work or by hearsay and tradition, of this fine craft. The mention of it with the quick understanding that to me, too, it was a thing of worth and importance, was an open sesame to their women's wisdom. One would tell how the cards were put into her hands as soon as she was old enough to sit alone and another would recollect that a thick plank was laid beside the spinning wheel so that she could learn to spin when too small to reach the wheel. Here and there a new bit of knowledge came to light, of the best ways of working wool and flax, or rules for coloring, of the dye plants, of how to draw in a selvedge that was sure to hold the threads in place in the pattern weaving; and in the house of every coverlet weaver there was always the bringing out of old drafts.

At first we tried out a number of these, having a short piece woven of each one. As this involved drawing each pattern through the harness, it was an expensive way to learn what each pattern was like. It seemed to me there must be some way of reading the drafts and by dint of "setting my head to it" I discovered that the patterns could be worked out on paper, with brush or crayon, giving a good idea of how the woven fabric would look. In this way over a hundred patterns were transferred to paper and we found out which were the best worth putting into the loom. We could tell also what patterns were similar under different names and with different parts or proportions.

As the enterprise developed it was a satisfaction to find that the three purposes that had been in mind from the start were in a way to fulfilment; to save the old arts from extinction; to give paying work to women too far from market to find it for themselves; and, more important than all, to bring interest into their lives, the joy of making useful and beautiful things. Out of it were coming more than these: for myself as well as for those engaged in the doing, friendships formed of enduring stuff, true homespun of the heart.

In the younger women who were learning to weave and keeping at it, I could see the growth of character. A slack-twisted person cannot make a success as a weaver of coverlets. Patience and perseverance are of the first necessity, and the exercise of these strengthen the fibers of the soul. Rhoda shed many tears over her first web, for the loom was old, and the material all flax, the hardest thread of all to manage for a warp when home spun. I had not seen the tears, but divined them and when, having persisted, she brought me the finished web it was worth to her and to me more than its weight in gold.

One who has had to do with hundreds of mountain girls in their teens has told me that never did she find one to be of weak and flabby character whose mother was a weaver; there was always something in the child to build on.

It was satisfactory, too, to notice how the money was spent that came in from the work. In one family one daughter after another had her chance at a good school because of the chance that her mother had to do paying work. In another there were many times when the weaving money was all that stood between little children and real hardship. In many it made all the difference between just enough and plenty. Cows were bought on money advanced to a steady worker and while the children thrived on the milk the mother "beat out" the pay at her loom.

Not all our looms were engaged in the weaving of coverlet designs. There were weavers of linsey, of whom one of the best was Mrs. Ann Shelton of Shelton-Laurel. During the winter she and her girls would prepare the yarn from her own sheep, washing, picking, dyeing part of the wool black or indigo blue, and mixing with white, carding this "mixtry" and spinning the yarn which for good linsey must be fine and even. The warp was left white for a light gray and for the darker colored cloth was dyed with maple bark or with hickory and copperas. The men of the family often made demands on the output of Ann's loom so that we felt ourselves favored if we could have some of the web for our orders.

In another part of Laurel (as the region in which Allanstand lies is called) were woven the Allanstand or Colonial blankets, using the "full-sleyed" linsey weave. These were made for couch covers with the cotton warp of white, the yarn filling sometimes of blue, with border stripes of white, and sometimes of browns or yellows and orange from the bark and leaf and flower dyes. At Allanstand had lived Aunt Polly Shelton, mother of sons and daughters, who left behind her many examples of her industry and skill. Among these were spreads embroidered in original designs with homespun thread. One of her daughters-in-law wove for us a cotton canvas and another embroidered this, copying designs. Gradually she made her own patterns, delighting in the work. Now her daughter-in-law, in her turn, carries on the tradition.

Rag rugs were made from the first, and in some of them a coverlet design is woven throughout, or as a border at each end, using the rags instead of wool thread to make the pattern. Silk rags are woven into runners and for curtains.

It was not long before we found tufted spreads in mountain homes that had been handed down from mother or grandmother, and later the knotted spreads were also made for our shop. The first of the "turfed" spreads that we marketed was copied from one made by Grandmother Duncan seventy years before. Her great grand-daughter, by whom the spread was treasured, was the maker of the one we sold. As far as I know, it was never afterwards copied. Grandmother Duncan was then living in Yancey County in a hale old age. She had designed the spread, using her own garden flowers as models.

The names of the knotted and tufted spreads are many. One of the most quaint is "Bird in the Tree." There are "Vines" of many sorts and "Bowls" and "Wreaths of Roses," a "Wreath" too for Napoleon. There are Bowknots and Flowers— garden flowers and wild ones.

At White Rock at the center of Laurel the women became famed for their appliqué quilt-tops, cut and sewed with exquisite care. The pieced quilts, too, when

Knotted Spread: "Bird in Tree."

The Chain or Warp as it is taken
from the Warping Bars.

Wool Cards.

Carding.

made in good patterns and color, found a market, but not as readily as the "patch-work," as the appliqué work is called.

The market for hooked rugs did not develop for some years, though from the first a few were made for us. Besides the more conventional patterns we have rugs sent to us with a whole dooryard depicted, hens as large as the houses, chickens of all colors, rabbits, horses and, of course, the universal cat.

Our first feather fans came to us from the mountains of Georgia. A few turkey fans are sent, but most of them are charming creations of duck feathers, from those of pure white to a mixture of soft gray or brown and white. The handles are wrought cleverly of the quills, adding much to the beauty of the fan. The most beautiful, however, are the large fans of peacock feathers.

Our venture in basket-making, which has grown to such large proportions, came almost by accident. A man who had become a cripple from rheumatism moved into Brittain's Cove, hoping to find help there in supporting his family. He had taken up the making of baskets and made good, firm, split baskets of the traditional melon shape. These he sold to his neighbors for the small sums they could afford to give him, but it was not an adequate wage for the work and unusual skill and care in-volved. Telling him that we could market his baskets at fair price if he would keep up to standard, improving in the smoothing of the splits, we took his whole output, which became considerable. He kept to his part of the bargain, and I look now in vain for baskets to match his, in shape and workmanship. He made a good support for his family as long as he lived. Though we had never seen color in a mountain basket, we suggested to this man to color some of the splits with a native dye and these, in brown and white, proved to be more marketable than the all-white baskets. I think it was chestnut-oak bark that we used first for the brown dye. As the years went on other basket-makers came in our way, a few other shapes were discovered and others evolved to make the great variety sold today.

From White Rock, Madison County, came the basket with squared ends which we named the White Rock basket. One man brought us our first boat or canoe basket, copied from the Indians, and some one else seeing it, evolved a "picking basket" by joining two canoes at one end, leaving the other ends wide apart. The basket is held in place against the waist of the picker by a thong around the neck.

In Munich one of us saw a basket which was just half of the melon basket, and this, suggested to the workers, was successfully made of splits and took its place as the Tyrol basket.

Kentucky furnished the pattern for the Jug basket or "Old Kentucky." A large flat oval shape was brought in one day and explained as the quill basket, used by weavers in old times to hold the quills for the shuttles. It is easy to see how the "Watermelon" got its name and the "Muzzle" and "Half-Muzzle." In the "Clover Basket" the ribs are so placed in the weaving that when closely made it will hold a seed as small as clover. There are over twenty shapes now on our list. The melon basket is made in all sizes from the big chip-basket for the hearth to the favors, two inches across.

The coloring is done mainly with native dyes, though some good commercial dyes are used. For the browns there is the red-oak bark which with copperas and alum and lye gives a ruddy brown. For a light brown take alder bark and alum and after the splits are colored, throw them into lye to set and darken. Another rule says, "Boil alder bark. To the strained ooze add salt and soda. But this is a dark brown." Sourwood bark and copperas give also a good brown dye and so do walnut roots.

A good worker tells us that wood to be well colored "must be boiled thirty minutes by clock with salt and soda used as mordant."

The "puccoon root" (blood root) is a fine dye for wood, a rich orange color, very valuable. Yellow root (Hydrastis) furnishes yellow; used with salt and with alum it makes a lemon yellow. Maple bark and white-oak bark and copperas give a blue. Any yellowish color dipped in lye turns purplish brown. "Gather mulberries when dead ripe, put berries on stove with barely enough water to cover them. Let boil, strain through cloth and dye the splits while still hot." You will have a purple or lavender.

This by no means exhausts the list.

Of the willow baskets the shapes are part traditional and part copied or originated. One of the favorite old designs is the cup and saucer and this is still made and sold, being suitable for holding flowers or a plant. There are work baskets, trays and favors and Grandma's cap basket, and a variety of other shapes. When left undyed, the willow gradually darkens to a deep brown. Boiling the withes in their own bark, or in onion skins, turns them to a silvery gray, which is permanent.

Soon after we had a salesroom in Asheville and a manager, she experimented with the honeysuckle vine which grows luxuriantly over the country side, for she had seen some notice of it as basket material in a government bulletin. She discovered how to prepare the vine, which is like a fine reed, not short like the willow withes, and handed the suggestion and the result of her experiments to a basket-maker living not far from town. This worker succeeded in weaving the vine into charming work baskets with covers, and hanging baskets to hold jars and vases of flowers. Coloring some of the vine with red and some with a green dye, she wrought into the baskets flowers and leaves of her own designing.

In the mountains, a woman who is crippled is very much to be pitied; usually no way is open to her save to be a burden on her men-folks. A young girl, who was too lame for field or garden work and even for much housework, was taught something of raffia-tying by a sojourner in her neighborhood, and seeing a basket of the long-leaved pine, she worked out the process for herself and became one of our steady contributors. The needles were sent her from the Eastern part of our long State, so that we were not departing from our custom of using native materials save in the raffia for binding the needles. She became not only a self-supporting woman but was able to help her parents as they grew older.

Bulrushes, growing in every swamp, can be woven into baskets and have been so used, time out of mind. Those made for the Industries are bound either in the old way, with a thin split, or with raffia.

The mountaineer, like the Yankee, has a bent for whittling and is never more happy than with knife in hand. Some charming models have come to us, tiny ploughs, sleds for logging, for gathering corn from steep fields where a wagon cannot go, and for many a use, not on ice and snow, but on dry ground about an uptilted farm. Spinning wheels, too; miniature looms, on which one could really make a fairy web; corn-stalk houses, of the old-style, two-story, log fashion; wagons, whittled out, just like the real thing and with canvas cover. All these are in addition to toys cut out of rhododendron wood, the tiny chairs, birdhouses, churns, whistles and paper knives that tempt the sojourner in Asheville. One of our workers in wood made boxes carved out of solid wood, and decorated them with cut-in designs, using at first his pocket knife and later fashioning himself knife blades to suit his need.

On the highways and byways of the southern mountains in the eighties and nineties one might meet at certain seasons of the year covered wagons with a name rudely painted on the canvas indicating the locality whence they came. The wagon-beds were filled with pottery, packed in straw and fresh from the kiln; jugs to hold whiskey or molasses; jars for pickles and for preserved fruit and wide-mouthed pitchers for household use. The driver of the pottery wagon, who was also the potter, peddled his wares from house to house, offering the jars and pitchers at 10 or 20 or 30 or 40 cents according to the number of gallons they would hold. He was a boon to the remote housewives who looked for this opportunity to replenish their equipment, and to the maker of moonshine he was not less welcome.

The ware he carried was serviceable, though rough, finished with a grey or brown or greenish glaze with little or no thought of beauty but sometimes achieving it to a remarkable degree.

Several potteries are now carried on with more knowledge and skill and with direct artistic purpose. Among their great variety of shape and color one finds also the old forms and the old glazes. Some of the best of this new-old pottery is always to be found in our shop, since we serve as an exchange for mountain crafts.

The business of marketing our products was for some years carried on from Allanstand, with the aid of an annual exhibition in Asheville. In 1908 we felt justified in opening a shop in Asheville, and in 1917 the business was incorporated, the by-laws providing that "no dividends should be paid the stockholders of over 6% per annum, but that all surplus above that should be turned into the business, or used for the benefit of the craftspeople of the mountains.

Most of the enterprises which have been successful in the reviving and marketing of craft work in the southern mountains, whether connected with a school or fostered by individual effort, have had beginnings similar to those of the Allanstand Cottage Industries. The secrets of handiwork, fast being forgotten, were learned from those who could still tell them, and the work produced for market was identical with what had been made for home or neighborhood use during several generations, or was a natural evolution of some old craft.

Two ventures, however, differ from these in that the work undertaken, though akin to mountain crafts, was not native to this mountain region. Of these two, therefore, the Biltmore Estate Industries, and the Tryon Toy Makers and Wood Carvers, there should be more than a brief mention.

With both of these Eleanor P. Vance and Charlotte L. Yale have been connected, so that the two industries are linked together by their common debt to these wise and gifted women.

THE BILTMORE ESTATE INDUSTRIES

OF the beginnings of the Biltmore Estate Industries Miss Yale writes:

> I cannot think of much to say about our beginnings. It all came about so naturally by doing the next thing. We went to Biltmore in 1901 and rented one of the little cottages. Since Miss Vance has always carved, she used the kitchen table as a work bench, carving for her own pleasure. Two or three small boys became interested visitors, so Miss Vance organized a Boys' Club with four members and taught them wood-carving, little realizing that she was making history, for she was the first to bring wood-carving to the section.
>
> Later, Dr. Swope, rector of All Soul's Church in Biltmore, asked us to be his Parish Visitors, and finally Mrs. George W. Vanderbilt became interested, and out of the little Club and the Church Work grew the Biltmore Estate Industries.

The first work undertaken for Mrs. Vanderbilt was the teaching of wood carving, and the classes were opened to girls as well as to boys, but only to young people who lived on the Biltmore Estate. The superintendent of the public schools of Asheville became interested and asked that a class be started in the high school. This was impossible with the plans that Mrs. Vanderbilt had in view and with the demands made on Miss Yale and Miss Vance by the growth and development of their classes. The attention of the Asheville superintendent once aroused, he secured a teacher and started what was perhaps the first class of manual training in the Asheville schools.

The wood carving at Biltmore naturally led to cabinetmaking. There was plenty of walnut and other good native woods in the Biltmore forests; and carving could be applied to furniture of good design and workmanship. A skilled cabinetmaker was brought from New York to instruct the class for a time, and by working themselves at night Miss Vance and Miss Yale became masters of the art and craft of woodworking. After this, no outside teaching was needed. With the training of eye and hand went also teaching the classes in the history of furniture and in design, giving a broad education in the craft.

The fact that Miss Vance is an artist and student of design had been from the first and throughout one of the chief assets of the school. It was her originality and gift that gave the designs used in carving their rare beauty. Motifs taken from the rhododendron and from the dogwood, so abundant in the mountain woods, were especially successful.

After Mrs. Vanderbilt saw the possibilities of the little Industrial School in which she had become so much interested, she determined to try to improve the method of hand weaving done by the people of the region in their homes. Since the weaving of coverlets had been already taken up by another agency, and could safely be left to develop in its hands, Mrs. Vanderbilt turned her attention to the producing of an all-wool fabric of the sort made in Scotland and especially in the Harris Islands, and much sought after for suitings. The two ladies in charge of the woodworking school undertook this new venture with fervor. It entailed numberless trips over the large Estate, visiting the women who could spin or card or weave; consulting with them, learning from them, setting them to work with equipment in use for generations on wool bought here and there from one and another of the farmers. At that time an experiment was being made on the estate in sheep raising, and the wool for the first essays in weaving came in part from the estate flock.

It was not usual for the weavers of the southern mountains to use a warp of wool. Even the blankets were woven on a cotton warp, so used as to allow the wool to be beaten up closely. Learning as they went, the teachers found that for the warp thread the yarn must be spun quite differently, and with a tighter, harder twist. For the filling it should be softer in order to beat up into the warp. No spinner could successfully prepare both kinds, alternately, so certain women were kept to the work of spinning warp yarn, others to making the yarn for filling. There were others still who wove the cloth, and we must not forget those who prepared the wool for spinning, by washing and carding it.

The method first tried was to have each process carried out in the home, from the washing of the wool through the various breakings, coloring with native dyes, mixing, carding, and spinning, until at last it went to the weaver who in her home also warped and beamed the warp and wove the fabric. This entailed endless delays and much carrying back and forth. Gradually the work was more and more centralized in the shop and school in Biltmore Village. There were a few women, however, who undertook the whole process and continued to supply a web now and then, till the business was sold and removed to Grove Park Inn.

Among the difficulties met with was the quality of the wool. It was found that spring wool and fall wool do not mix with good result; that buying in small lots was unsatisfactory when a cloth of uniform quality and texture was not only desirable but imperative, if the work was to be put on a business basis. This basis itself was necessary to make the undertaking one of real use and profit to the workers.

There were other difficulties. It was easier to find weavers than to provide yarn for them, for the spinning, and, above all, the carding gave "misery in the shoulders." There was at that time a small mill, run by water power, on Reems Creek, near Weaverville, where so-called homespun was produced of a rough but durable quality. To the wise Scotchman who owned and ran the mill the teachers applied, and, since he was ready to close out his business, they purchased from him the old set of cards, small according to modern ideas, and greatly worn and moth-eaten. This, however, when set up in Biltmore in Mr. Vanderbilt's own car shed, given up for the purpose, seemed wonderful to the force at work. There it was fitted with electric power and did the work well, with great relief to aching shoulders. The worn condition of the cards was found to be an asset, giving to the yarn something of the quality obtained by hand carding, which is usually lost by using machinery.

Still the product of the Biltmore looms was not up to the standard set by Mrs. Vanderbilt and her helpers. It was rough and had not the softness and finish of the homespun of Ireland and the Scottish islands. It could not yet be accepted by the tailors. So Miss Vance and Miss Yale were sent to the British Isles. There with the pertinacity and acumen they have always shown, they found the secrets of the failure. Their yarn was made of the wool of sheep allowed to have the run of the woods and pastures, where tiny burrs and prickers and minute bits of thorn adhered to the fleeces and could not be got rid of by any known process. The sheep in the old country were kept in inclosures, free from briers and thorns. Another source of failure was an imperfect method of washing the wool. The teachers learned the whole process, from the sheep's back to the finished fabric, and came home to put it in practice.

It was necessary in order to bring the Biltmore Homespuns to perfection to abandon the buying of country wool, and to order from the large wool growers. One of the old hand looms, one hundred years old, was brought from Scotland to Biltmore Village to serve as a model for others to be made by the boys of the woodworking class. It is now set up as a keepsake in the Homespun Shop. It is worth noting here that the cards used in one of the most successful weaving establishments in Scotland were as moth-eaten and worn as the old set purchased from the mill on Reems Creek.

In regard to the old loom from Scotland, Miss Yale says:

It differed from ours in one point only: it had a fly shuttle, which made it possible to produce more yards in a day with less strain on the weaver. When we took this loom to the older people on the Estate, at the time some of them being in their nineties, they recalled that the old looms which they had probably brought from the old country with them originally had the fly shuttles. As so often happens in this section, the fly shuttle needed repair and they just drifted along without it, finally going back to the old way of pushing the shuttle through by hand.*

Two guiding principles in the minds of Miss Vance and Miss Yale are responsible for the success of the Industries on the Biltmore Estate: To be satisfied with nothing short of the best; and to go to the bottom of every failure or difficulty. By carrying out these principles they have done something of far greater worth than the building up of a craft industry. They have built up character in the young people who have had the chance to work under their charge. Too often they were inclined to "crumple up," as Miss Yale puts it, under a difficulty. This was true also of the older workers. For instance: a piece of cloth was brought in during the early days of the weaving industry with a sleazy strip an inch wide running the length of the web. It was pointed out to the weaver. Yes, she knew it was there, had seen it all along, but she didn't know what to do about it. "It just happened so." When it was suggested that there must be a cause and that she herself would not like to have such a web sold her, if she had ordered good cloth, she set her mind to work and discovered that a worn place in her reed had made the trouble. The new impetus given her that day was worth more than the substantial returns for her work, if we hold that the life is more than meat.

One thing at Biltmore led to another. For the carved chest there must be hinges and locks, and these must not be makeshifts but exactly suited to the style of the chests. Failing to find what was fitting among manufactured articles, the boys were taught to make what was needed. A beautiful

---

* The author differs from Miss Yale, believing that the fly-shuttle loom was the exception rather than the rule among the colonists.

pair of carved bellows was designed by Miss Vance, but lacked a nozzle; a hose nozzle was suggested and tried, but it was just a hose nozzle. A turning lathe for metal was procured and the boys, accustomed to the turning of wood, found that they could turn the nozzles of Miss Vance's designing out of solid brass. So began the metal-working shop.

The workers were not the only ones who needed and received teaching. The public received it as well. Sometimes an hour would be spent in showing an interested but ignorant customer what made the difference between one of the handmade stools with its perfection of joining and its good lines, and a jerry-made bit of furniture which could be turned out by the thousands. It all counted in the day's work, and such customers often returned and showed that the lesson had gone to heart and had been shared with others.

The Industries were maintained by Mrs. Vanderbilt until 1917, when they were sold to Mr. F. L. Seely, who has since then carried them on in Asheville under the name of The Biltmore Industries.

THE STORY OF THE TOY MAKERS AND WOOD CARVERS OF TRYON

In the year 1915 Eleanor P. Vance and Charlotte L. Yale came to Tryon, North Carolina, to make their home. They had laid the foundations of the Biltmore Industries, an accomplishment which might well suffice for a lifetime, but these women had full energy and zest left for some new undertaking. "The world is big enough," said they, "let's think up something else." Soon the Toy Makers of Tryon were at work.

Gathering together some of the young people of the neighborhood, they set these boys and girls to making the charming toys designed by Miss Vance. Not all who came to learn remained as makers of the toys, for from the first a high standard was set. Dozens of young people have come and gone again, unable to fit in to work that demands the unusual combination of artistic feeling, a quick eye, and a clever hand. Those who keep on do so because of an impulse within themselves which is satisfied with work like this. A few are conscious of this leaning beforehand, others find it out after they get into the atmosphere of the Toy Makers. Is it any wonder that the toys have a freshness and an originality never to be matched in a cut-and-dried factory? The work, being creative, is an inspiration to those who make and to those who see them. Someone called them "toys with souls." To quote from a published article:

The Noah's Ark is enough to grip the imagination of any navigator, not to mention its power over the heart of a child. The circus sets, complete with funny clowns, pink lemonade stands and a most joyously rotund fat lady, demand small excited hands to fondle them. Little Red Riding Hood walks forth with her faithless wolf, and little Bo-Peep waves her crook over numberless fleecy sheep; Simple Simon pleads for pies off a pieman's tray, and a long procession of nursery rhyme celebrities stand at attention, waiting for Santa Claus.

There are, besides, balancing elephants and workable churns, many colored tops, and some delightful book-ends that would grace the most fastidious nursery—snow-white bunnies with lovely pink eyes, that crouch low while holding the juvenile classics. Then there are prairie schooners with wide canvas tops, and sturdy oxen which look staunch enough to stand any kind of transcontinental journey, and play-cabins, carefully dove-tailed at the corners, like the huts of the pioneers, which open and shut with a precision that would delight a fresh-air fiend. The treasure trunks, copied after an ancient jewel-box out of another generation, are resplendent with all the airy forms of butterflies and flowers that the most imaginative child could desire; the prim little dolls in pinafores stand waiting for the protection of motherly girls who may choose them according to their frocks of pink or blue or lavender.

When the making of toys was well established, it was an easy step to the teaching of wood carving. Through the courtesy of Mr. Seely, this was made possible without infringing on the domain of the Biltmore Industries, then carried on at Grove Park Inn.

Miss Vance and Miss Yale have long felt that these southern mountains might produce future generations of wood carvers and toy makers such as are found in the mountain regions of Europe. Though the work is yet in its infancy, marked aptitude has been discovered and the originators feel encouraged. One of them says: "Wood-carving is genuine sculpture, in which every line and contour are carefully tooled by trained hands; in which fine material is applied to its noblest use; in which an ancient craft is followed with sincere fidelity and the highest creative aspirations."

So is established now the School and Business of the Tryon Toy Makers and Wood Carvers, where honest work is honored, the feeling for beauty given expression, and where character is made.

PART II. THE PEOPLE

The longer on this earth we live,
And weigh the various qualities of men,
Seeing how most are fugitive
Or fitful gifts at best of now and then
Wind-wavered, corpse-lights, daughters of the fen,
The more we feel the high, stern-featured beauty
Of plain devotedness to duty,
Steadfast and still, nor paid with mortal praise.
But finding amplest recompense
For life's ungarlanded expense
In work done squarely and unwasted days.

JAMES RUSSELL LOWELL

I believe in working, then a body has something.

AUNT LIZA

It's as near honor to work as anything that ever was done.

GRANNY JUDE

1. A SPINNER

WHEN I first saw Aunt Liza she was "upwards in sixty," but still strong and active, with brisk step and bright eyes. Later the strength was weakened and the step more slow, but to the end of her days the spirit within her looked out of those gray eyes with the keen interest in things and in people which was her birthright.

One hot afternoon in July I started out from the cluster of houses where I was spending a few weeks of leisure in a busy year. Tired of my usual ride on the road that wound through the valley, I struck off over the hill to the Big Cove. There a sidetrack through a thicket of rhododendrons beguiled me and turning "Lady's" head to the left, I plunged into the green gloom.

Soon the trail began to ascend, winding around the steep side of the Cove. It was a rough cart track, washed by rains and furrowed by the logs "snaked down" to the saw yard below. The trees stood close on either side, with feathery undergrowth and pale forest blossoms.

"Only a logging road," I thought to myself, "we shall soon come to the end," but still the road climbed on, till, of a sudden, we came out into bright sunshine, and there, high up on a bench of the mountain side, between the great summit above and the deep Cove below, was a clearing, a field of corn, a patch of sorghum, and the quaintest of cabins. Even in the first glance an air of thrift was noticeable, the garden fence of rived palings was without a break, there were no tall weeds about the house, but flowers made a blaze of color against the gray of logs and shingles.

Tying "Lady" at the edge of the woods I stepped forward and saw, coming from the spring beyond the house, Aunt Liza. We met, and looking one another in the eyes, took stock each of the other, and then and there our friendship began.

She had been hoeing corn and part of her little crop had been "laid by" for the year; but with her natural courtesy she begged me to sit with her "a spell." "It won't bother me one mite, it'll give me a chance to rest up," she said.

Sitting on the vine-wreathed porch we talked about the place where she had lived so long. She had come to it a bride, she told me, riding behind her husband on the mule that was their one valuable possession. She described to me the summer dawns and the nights and her delight in them.

"It's mighty pretty and it puts feelings on to a body to see the moon-shine falling on yon mountain. I just naturally love moonshine. I don't know, either, but what I like it here full as well along about daylight, when I'm up soon of a morning and the sky ferninst is all the color of them roses yonder. Here right lately there's been the prettiest kind of a big star, seems like it sorter hates to go out of sight at sun-up."

We went about the little yard, fenced in to keep the chickens from "tear-ing up the pretties." The gourd vine on the fence was planted, she explained, to keep out snakes, who dislike the smell of these vines.

"The gourds are mighty handy things to have and my children always look for me to raise them some. There's a sort of a knack about raising gourds, some folks can't have no luck with 'em, 'pears like."

We compared our nomenclature: she called the cosmos, making ready to bloom, "flying ciphers," and the "pretty boys" that flourished in the fence corners, were, in my dictionary, zinnias.

She showed me with pride the little crop. "Ever since my old man died I've made enough corn to do me, and sweetening too. The boys they come and plough for me in the spring of the year; they'd be willing to do more than that, but I believe in working, then a body has something."

This was the first of many visits to the "Swallow's Nest," as I named it. We exchanged confidences; for Aunt Liza was as eager to hear of the world known to me as I to know about her world. She was filled not with a vain longing for unknown paths, but with an intense delight in the one she was traveling and an interest in those of which she could catch glimpses from other people. A description of a large department store with its moving staircase and elevators gave her food for thought.

"They must be scary things, them rooms that tote you to the top of the house," she said, "reckon I'd yell when they go to start. The scariest thing ever I see was an engine. My old man, he had me to go down to the railroad with him once and I see two trains go by, a passenger and a freight. I don't know as I'd want to risk my old bones in any such as that, but I 'low it's just as natural to you as sitting in your own dooryard. It's just in the way a body's raised."

Early or late, my visits never found Aunt Liza idle. Often as I climbed the bars, the hum of the spinning wheel would come from the cabin; some-times a lonesome hymn tune sung in a high-pitched, quavering voice, floated down from the hillside where she was gathering berries for winter use.

How much I learned that summer! Aunt Liza said I did "mighty well for the chaince" I'd had in my "raising." It was a proud moment for us both when the wool cards, so docile in her hands and so bewitched in mine, at last made for me a roll that could be spun; and again when I drew out on the big wheel a thread that was not too uneven. One day I was taught to make the crisp, wholesome corn pones for our dinner, baking them in the iron oven on the hearth.

"Are you never afraid, up here alone?" I asked her once.

"What is there to be afeard of, honey?" she rejoined. "There's snakes, of course, rattlers, out on the ridge, but they don't come about the place now like they used to. They was bears here, too, when we first come; they used to get our hogs and our young calves. My old man always took his gun with him whenever he'd go off anywheres from the house.

"I reckon you want to know how come us to settle in such a fur off place. We was both young then and we hadn't nothing to start in on, the ground was good and to be had for the clearing; we could make a heap of truck. It suited us too. Since their paw's dead and I'm getting up in years, 'pears like it makes the children plumb uneasy for me to be here by myself; they're always and forever at me to come and live amongst 'em. One of my daughters is married to a mighty nice man. He's a good provider, and they've built them an awful fine house down in the flat-woods. It's a main big-un. It's got six rooms in it and some other little rooms where she keeps her plunder; calls 'em closets. But seems like I can't be satisfied anywheres else than here. 'Taint like home, I tell them.

"Reckon I'm quare-turned and ill," she said, turning to me with a mischievous gleam in her eye, "but I can't stand it to live with any of 'em, leastways with my daughters-in-law; they're good women, too, but folks has their ways. It frets me, too, to have such a passel of young-uns about; I can't be devilled with 'em. Up here I ain't no botherments at all. I'm always at work at something or another and I ain't no time to set and study about them that's gone; that's what makes a body lonesome."

In spite of this desire for solitude, Aunt Liza was a factor in the life of the neighborhood. Her children made frequent visits, and she was called on as a matter of course to help whenever there was a "working"; whether "fodder pulling," "corn shucking," or "grubbing"; for no one else could superintend as she could the cooking of a big dinner. As a friend to be depended on in sickness or other trouble, she had everyone's good word.

After that summer it was many years before I turned my face back to the mountains. When again settled in the old quarters, I took my way up the well-remembered trail. The neighbors had told me that Aunt Liza had been asking about my coming and would be "proud" to see me.

As I approached, she was sitting on the porch and though a light flashed in her eyes for a moment, all she said was, "Git in, git you a cheer," but after we had talked a little of indifferent things, she said, "You was gone so long I thought I was never going to see you no more.

"I'm right sharply decayed since you saw me," she added, pulling up a sleeve to show her shrunken arm, "I can't do much work and that frets me, but I ain't a punishing any; a body ought to be thankful for that."

A shy smiling little maiden stayed with her great-grandmother now, and the child's father came every few days to split the wood and to do other work too heavy for little Loduska.

Aunt Liza's fingers were not too feeble to use the knitting needles, and their clicking made a cheerful accompaniment to our talk. I had a tale to tell of foreign lands, which had to be continued from visit to visit.

"Shucks! You don't tell me!" she would exclaim with a whack on my knee, at hearing of some strange custom. "It does beat all, what humans will do. D'ye reckon our ways would seem as quare to them?"

There had been more time to "study" as Aunt Liza sat by the fire through the long winter days and I heard more of old times and the husband dead for twenty years, and of the children and grandchildren scattered abroad. Of her children there were ten living; I knew many of them and had knowledge of them all, stalwart, honest men and women. Some of them were living plainly as their parents had done; others had fought their way to easier circumstances. Among the grandchildren there were two who had gone out into the world beyond the mountains to use gifts of no mean value.

And all looked to the old woman on the mountain side with veneration; from her had gone forth the law by which they lived; the law of straight dealing and kindness.

On my return to the mountains the following summer my first question to my hosts was of Aunt Liza. They told me that my friend was gone.

One lovely summer afternoon I made a pilgrimage to the spot where we had known and loved each other. The cabin was deserted, the half-open door showed an empty room, in the garden weeds strove with the flowers.

Climbing the ridge behind the house, I reached the little inclosure where there were now two graves instead of one. Busied with memories, I sat there in the twilight till the moon rose over the opposite mountain and flooded Aunt Liza's beloved hillside with light.

2. BLACK SHEEP'S WOOL

THE Weaving-Woman had been warned against taking the trip just then. It was early in April, and for six weeks the rains had descended. Disaster was prophesied; the party would be mired in the clay roads; would meet with washouts in the mountains and run the risk of drowning in the fords of the mountain creeks. The Weaving-Woman and the Captain and the Captain's wife would not hear to reason, though every friend they met told them it couldn't be done. In a stout carryall with two good mules they were doing it.

The waters were high just as they had been told, and when they came to the bad ford where a V turn was to be made in midstream to avoid a huge, slippery rock, they had their one real scare. The carryall tipped dangerously as the wheels struck the rock, and the stream overflowed the bed of the wagon. The Captain's wife, in that moment of uncertainty, being of a practical turn, reached down and snatched up the basket that held the bread, for she felt, rather than thought, that if they didn't drown after all it would be desirable to have it unsoaked with creek water.

They were not drowned; the mules struggled valiantly with the rocks and the swift current, and drew them to the bank in safety. The others were glad that the bread was dry, though they laughed at the Captain's wife for remembering it at that serious moment.

It was then that they decided the mules deserved to be "brevetted horses," like those mentioned long ago in an army dispatch.

Toward nightfall the party was safely through the many fords of Roaring Creek and was crossing the watershed. Coming to a fork they were uncertain which road to take. It was a lonely spot, a little flat with heavily wooded hills at either hand and with no sign of human habitation. While they were consulting a makeshift map, a woman was seen entering the woods to the right, a big basket on her arm, a child running by her side.

The Captain jumped from the wagon and hastening across the open ground asked the way to Randolph. With speed greater than his, the woman and girl fled through an opening in the trees. The Captain followed till he lost sight of them where a splashing waterfall poured down from the rocks and almost barred the trail. As he mounted his seat again, he asked meditatively, "Could they have taken us for revenue officers?"

Some months later the Weaving-Woman was again in that part of the mountains. Her name had not been given her by her friends because she herself wove, but because she was continually encouraging others to do so. Just now she was in search of yarn.

Her friends in the neighborhood told her of the stores of wool usually on hand at the Fox house, "the Lem Fox house." On her pony she rode up the valley of Roaring Creek. The stream, so full and tumultuous in April, was shrunken out of recognition. Instead of budding trees and shy, spring flowers, she saw the rich colors of autumn.

Soon she found herself again in the Hollow Gap, crossing the flat at the watershed and searching for the path to the right up which had fled the startled pair on her first trip. Her pony picked his way up the trail, past the waterfall and on through heavy woods to a clearing. At the farther and upper side stood the Fox house in a space bare of trees, a garden patch beside it and a cornfield below, bare now, in October, of all but stalks.

The house was built of squared logs and was tall and gaunt and lonesome looking. It commanded perfectly the approach. The very clutter on the porch: saddles, gears, spinning wheel, bundles of beans, dried or drying, spoke of a place seldom visited by strangers.

The one large room was lighted by the two open doorways. At the left as one entered from the road, a fire burned in a large fireplace and on the sticks rested a kettle boiling fiercely. The Weaving-Woman guessed that in it was the dinner of beans and bacon.

There was an air of unfriendliness in the reception she met with from Mrs. Fox that she was unused to. It changed to one of armed neutrality when she told where she came from and again to something like real welcome when she named friends of both of them and explained her errand.

In the open doorway opposite to that by which she had entered stood a churn, and against the door jamb leaned a little girl in a bright, homemade linsey dress that reached nearly to the floor. She was eating a raw turnip with relish and looking at the stranger with frank curiosity.

When her mother had gone out to a shed to hunt up the wool and yarn that could be spared, she drew nearer to the visitor, ready to answer questions about herself.

"What do you study in school?"

"Bluebackspeller!"*

"Anything else?"

"The Testament."

---

*Noah Webster's Bluebacked Spelling Book was in use in the southern mountains up to the beginning of this century. In some schools it was the only textbook except the New Testament.

"Yes," she had one sister who went to school with her, "but Donia," indicating with a gesture the empty chair beside the churn, "she's too old to go. She's fifteen, goin' on sixteen. She's talkin' to Jem Taylor. She's too growed up to be goin' to school."

It was some minutes before it dawned upon the mind of the Weaving-Woman that "talking" to a boy meant "keeping company" with him.

The child came still nearer to the Weaving-Woman: "There's our *cake of soap*," she said, and pointed to a little shelf.

Sure enough, there it was, and it was pink.

Just then Mrs. Fox came in and with her came Donia, both of them laden with bundles of wool and hanks of yarn.

"It takes a heap of wool to do us," said Mrs. Fox, "what with all the men-folks goes through in a year, and for blankets, and for us a coat* apiece."

In one corner of the room stood the loom and in it was a web of jeans, dark brown. The Weaving-Woman could see that it was being woven of black sheep's wool. Could she have some yarn like that? But there was only enough to finish out the pattern for a man's suit.

"It's for my eldest boy, he's in Randolph jail for sellin' blockade whiskey," Mrs. Fox explained, with no thought of being ashamed nor of the appropriateness of the garments she was fashioning for her son.

"He's been in there now four months."

"So," thought the Weaving-Woman, "six months ago the boy was at liberty, and his mother had reason to dread the sight of strangers and to run to give the alarm."

"My son in jail and his wife bad off!" continued Mrs. Fox. "There's one thing I neen'ter worry about now; when he's in jail he can't be killed or crippled in a fight with them revenues. All the time he's out I have a dread on me."

Though she was the most unsuspicious of persons, a weird feeling took hold of the visitor that there was someone else in the house. Did she hear the faintest creaking of a board overhead? Or was it imagination?

While Mrs. Fox had stepped outside on some errand, little Opal said to her sister, "What for did you tell me Paw warn't at home? You know he is," and was promptly hushed up.

To the Weaving-Woman's aroused fancy, there was a man crouching behind the door on the stair that led to the loft above them, perchance with

---

* Coat = petticoat.

shotgun in hand. It was none of her business, however, and she said good-bye to Mrs. Fox with sincere expressions of good will on both sides.

Donia said she would go a piece with her. Had there been a signal between her and her mother?

At the fence they found the pony with bridle broken in her efforts to crop some inviting bits of grass. Donia stepped to a shed and producing a home-tanned squirrel skin cut from it a narrow strip. This she twisted deftly and with it repaired the bridle.

"There now," said she, "that's twict as strong as 'twas before; squirrel hide is the lastin'est thing there is for to make a body a string."

Down the hollow they went, deep in conversation. The Weaving-Woman walking and leading her horse that she and Donia might talk the more easily. They talked of Randolph and the many sights there; of railway engines; Donia allowed she "loved to hear 'em holler when they got near the station. Even here in the Hollow Gap," she said, "we can hear 'em exhortin' miles and miles away in the flat-lands, just afore it commences to rain."

Out on the big road, the Weaving-Woman mounted and rode away. As she looked back before the road turned, she saw Donia still standing at her post watching her out of sight.

"Wal, did ye see old man Fox, when ye was up to his place?" said someone to the Weaving-Woman on her return to the little settlement where she was sojourning; "reckon they didn't show you the still, but you must have passed within ten feet of it, goin' and comin'."

3. A LINSEY-WOOLSEY DRESS

LOIS RICE is off on an adventure: to teach the school on Middle-Lonesome. Fresh from her own training and her graduation day, she is leaving her home, a small mountain town, for the first time. Middle-Lonesome is to be her first school and her first venture into the world. Though she is stout-hearted, there are moments when all her courage is needed, and when the task before her wears an aspect more terrifying than alluring.

Lonesome Creek flows through a wilder part of the mountains than she has ever seen before, and the beauty of the woods and the streams as the mules plod on, over the hills and through many fords, makes her heart lighter.

Beside her, on the seat of the heavy mountain wagon, guiding the mules more by voice than by rein, sits Enoch Chalmers; "Shadrach's Enoch," to distinguish him from sundry cousins of the name. He is much bigger than Lois, but still of school age and one of her future scholars. There is time to get acquainted as they jog along at a pace of three miles an hour. Lois learns that there are ten children in the Shadrach Chalmers family.

"They're bouncin' to come to school," said Enoch. "They'll be there every last one of them, rain or shine. Paw's put him a handrail on our foot log so's even the least-un can cross when the creek's up."

Lois thinks that she will be sure of a school, whatever happens to the other children in the district.

She knows that her own salary of twenty-five dollars a month (an immense sum to her mind) is provided by the county, and that the fund for Middle-Lonesome allows a four months' session. From Enoch she learns how the people have been working since corn was "laid by" to provide a schoolhouse. Everybody in the settlement has had a hand in it, all giving work and some furnishing materials as well.

"Paw, he's givin' the land and he's hauled the brick from the railroad for the chimney. They've even made 'em up money enough for to get 'em *glass windows*. It's a mighty fine house; a complete thing," said Enoch, triumphantly.

As they reach the Poplar Gap and begin to descend to the creek, the mules quicken their pace, knowing well that home is near. Sounds of hammer and saw are heard, and soon, as they round a curve and come out into cleared land, Lois sees the neat frame building and a group of men giving the finishing touches.

The first to come forward to greet her is Jim Wilder, a patriarchal figure, tall and broad shouldered and bearded. His loud voice rolls on and on as he tells her, as he has been telling his fellow citizens, how proud he is that they are to have a teacher and a school right "at them," and foretells the great things that will happen for the good of the settlement.

Beside him stands Shadrach Chalmers, not less tall, stroking his black beard and smiling happily. His words are few, but to Lois they seem to mean more than the many words of Wilder, and she notices, even at this first meeting, that what he says carries weight with his neighbors.

Enoch's promise was made good. Shadrach's "ten" were in the school-yard every morning when school "took up" and when Lois, for lack of a bell, pounded on the side of the door, calling "Books! Books! Books!" There were many other scholars, for it is in August and September, between the last hoeing of corn and the beginning of fodder pulling, that a district school in the mountains best flourishes.

As long as the warm weather held, the girls' dresses were made of "cotton checks" also called "Alamance." Their skirts, reaching to their ankles, made them look to Lois like small editions of their mothers. The boys wore shirts of the same Alamance gingham, with long trousers of denim or of the linsey or jeans from the home looms. Later in the fall, the boys and girls would all be clothed with the durable homespun and home-woven fabrics, for in winter in the mountains there is no better wear.

With such a flock of pupils, Lois was often put to it to find room for all, and at times a row of the "least-uns" was seated on the edge of the platform, where they squirmed about at their ease.

Teaching an ungraded school of pupils whose ages range from six to twenty-one years is a test of the acid sort, and sometimes four o'clock in the afternoon found the little teacher's courage at a low ebb.

On the first day of school, when Shadrach Chalmers, as head of the school committee, had opened the house and had installed her formally, he had said to her: "Come over to the house some day soon and tell them you're at home." One evening after the schoolhouse had been swept as usual by two of the girls, Lois locked the door and went with Esther and Randy Chalmers over the foot log and up the lane between the fields of corn to the large log house, standing fenced in its dooryard. The yard was green with "yard grass" and gay with marigolds and zinnias. On the porch stood Mrs. Chalmers (Martha to all the neighborhood), strong, capable, and kind, with welcoming face for "teacher." Lois felt herself indeed at home with these people, so kindly and simple were they, so like her own people in the things that count.

As the two sat together on the porch, Mrs. Chalmers, like a good general, saw to it that her girls and boys were doing each his evening task, her own fingers busy the while with a half-knitted sock.

The talk at first was of indifferent subjects, but as the sun grew low, Mrs. Chalmers spoke of the great desire she and her husband had had to see a school near them and to have a good teacher who would "lead the children to think further, and cause them to take a straight course in doing right." Not long before this their eldest son, then "just turned of nineteen, had got to going with a rowdy set, and in one of their frolics he was shot dead."

"He's buried up on yon hill forninst us. The Chalmers' graveyard is down the creek a piece, but nothing would do his paw but to have his grave made up here. Shad used to sit on this porch and watch for him to come home over that hill."

The story was told with no least show of emotion nor bid for sympathy. For this very reason it brought to Lois a sense of the heavy and enduring grief behind it.

There was silence between the two for some minutes before Martha resumed. "Shad, he's mightily holp up about the school. He says as soon as he looked into those brown eyes of yourn he was plumb certin you was the teacher we was wantin'. No night would be too dark for him to come to your help, if so be you was needing hit."

To herself Lois said, "I'll succeed or be found trying."

Her quarters were with the Wilders. In a fine new house, for which the house pattern had been sawed out of Jim's own timber, she had the luxury of a room to herself.

As the days went on many comments on the school were reported to her, not all favorable.

"The wife doesn't get through braggin' on the school," said Jim one night; "she says you're the most *painful* teacher for the little fellows we've ever had in this country; but they's some 'lows you'll never make an out of it lessn you use the hickory on some of them rough boys. They want you should bresh 'em good."

Jim's mother-in-law, Peaceable Tim's widow, added her word. "You cain't please 'em all, comin' and goin'; here's Sam Saunders a tellin' it that you scorched his Sue Ollie t'other day. She's his pleasure-piece. Good land! I wisht ye'd a beat them boys of his to a frazzle. They sure is the aggavatinest young-uns in these parts."

"You neenter mind what all that feller Sam says," put in Jim, "he's just a bloodthirsty, ornary critter; doggone it!"

In the evenings after supper as the neighbors dropped in on errands or just to pass the time of day, Lois heard much talk and much complaint about the new stock law, lately adopted in the county, and learned that, before this, stock of all kinds was free to roam and feed at large. Crops were to be fenced against them and securely, for no damages for incursions could be charged. Now as the country was becoming thickly settled and moving out of the pioneer stage, the obnoxious law had come and it was the cattle who were to be fenced in at the risk of fines and lawsuits.

"It's got so," said Granny Jude, "that a pore body that hain't got no land cain't have no stock, and that's not right, I'm tellin' ye."

"Is it because of the stock law," said Lois, "that the Lansings have a gate in front of their house and no fence at all? I've seen fences without gates many a time but never before a gate standing all by itself."

"Yeah," said a neighbor scornfully, "Tom Lansing thinks that law is a going to pertect his dooryard. He's a powerful lazy critter and the fence was mighty handy for kinlin' wood. When Bob Greer's cow gets out, *accidental like*, mind you, I reckon Tom thinks the law'll rise right up and head her off. After she's et up them pretties of Mis Lansing's there ain't goin' to be any money that'll pacify his old woman. She'll be a rarin' and a ragin'."

"Let alone that they couldn't anybody collect money off'n Greer," said another of the group.

But the question treated seriously in these evening gatherings was that of the sheep and it was agreed that dogs *and* the stock law were about to make an end of sheep raising for all but the largest landowners.

Shad Chalmers, it was said, would keep right on. "He has a knack with him about stock, and his land lies right for the sheep."

Though in time the teacher visited the home of every one of her pupils, and made many friends among the neighbor women, it was to the Chalmers house that she went most often and with the most pleasure. There were many things about a mountain farm and many ways that were new to her and that she watched and entered into with zest. In the twilight of early fall she went with Martha to the "milk-gap," the pasture bars, where the cows gathered to be milked, and learned from her a new name for Orion: "the Milking Stars," as night after night the constellation rose in the south-

The Foot Log.

Middle-Lonesome School.

If anyone "cusses" his dog, right
then he's insulted.

After school hours.

The Mail Carrier.

Granny Jude's Cabin.

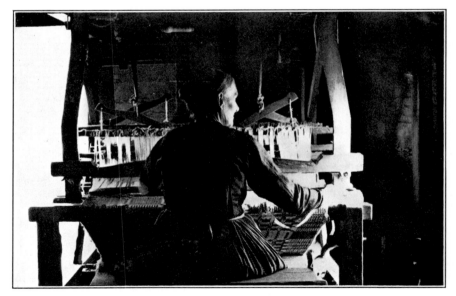

Granny Jude at work.

east at milking time. Better still she liked to go with Randy or Emmie up on the mountain to help salt the sheep or to drive them to the lower field.

In a tiny log house near the Big House, stood the loom with its appurtenances, idle now, for the autumn days were too full with the gathering and caring for the crop; the molasses making; the boiling of apple and pumpkin butter; the pickling of beans and kraut and the drying of pumpkin and squash to allow Martha time for weaving. In spite of the help her girls could give, she often felt as did Caesar of old when all things were to be done by him at once, and would exclaim, "Every turn's Martha's!"

Lois, looking at the sheep and then at the stores of coverlets and blankets on shelves reaching from the floor of the big room to the ceiling, wondered what were the processes by which the wool was converted into these fabrics and into the linsey and jeans with which the whole family was clothed.

It happened that the work was begun on a Saturday when all the children could help, and Lois saw the sheep driven into a shallow place in the creek to be washed and then she watched the men clip the trembling beasts, lying on a rough table with feet tied together. How small they looked as they ran off bleating, released of their heavy weight of wool.

"Some shears only once a year," said Martha, "but I sure do pity them that has the wool to work up; it's long and torn with briers and all matted up with burrs and trash. It loses more in the picking, too. I despise such as that."

Once off the sheep's back the wool was washed again, and on the thoroughness with which this was done depended much of the quality of the cloth. Spread out on the roof of low outhouses and on frames, it was left to dry.

Next began the "picking." Every bit of wool must be picked over to rid it of burrs and bits of weed. This was the task in the Chalmers family of the younger girls, and a task not popular, but under Martha's firm management there was no grumbling. When "picked" a white, fluffy mass, it had lost much of its weight.

Unless it was to be "dyed in the wool," it was then greased with lard, to make it possible to card and spin it. Long before all the wool was "picked" the carders began to work. Most of the girls were experts, the cards having been put into their hands as soon as they were old enough to hold them, but carding, even to those most accustomed to the work, is a wearisome job and hard on the shoulders. In the Chalmers home much of it was done as the family sat around the hearth at night, when the talk and the old tales and the singing of "song-ballets" lessened the tedium and made the workers forget their fatigue.

During those fall days the blue pot stood in the kitchen fireplace, keeping "about so warm," day and night, till the mixture had duly fermented and the color had "come."

Before the four months of school were over, the spinning wheel was going, turning the "rolls" as they came from the carders into skeins of even, smooth yarn. In fine weather the big wheel was carried out into the yard, near the wooden trough into which ran water, brought down from the spring on the mountain through pipes of logs. The cool sound of running water never ceased and made an accompaniment to the intermittent hum of the wheel.

Martha was famous throughout the region for her linsey-woolsey. There were no "bobbles" in it, nor uneven places nor broken selvedges. The webs that came from her loom were smooth and uniform and substantial. Of all the samples she had seen, Lois liked best a pure, light gray, of white wool with a little black wool "broken into" it; not black sheep's wool, which is brown, but a rich velvety black, dyed with walnut roots. "That cloth would make a coatsuit that could be worn anywhere," said Lois, "that would be my choice."

In school as on the farm, honest work had been done. It was with a good conscience one October day that Lois started with a bevy of the older pupils to attend a Singing Contest, yon side of the Lonesome Mountain. A singing teacher had been holding a school at Sugar Grove for two weeks and the singers had challenged the neighboring districts to bring along their shaped-note songbooks and sing them down if they could. Most of the party walked, keeping the same steady stride uphill and down and rarely letting the riders outgo them. To Lois, as an unaccustomed rider, had been given Moll, Jim Wilder's old brown mule. As she mounted, Mrs. Wilder said reassuringly, "Jest you set down on old Moll and keep on a settin' and you'll git thar."

That was a day to remember; the leisurely ride through the autumn woods; the red of sourwood and gum trees and the yellow of sugar maples, set off by the dark green of the pines and laurels; the glimpses, as they rounded the shoulder of some hill, of far-off hills blue in haze; the bustle of arrival at the Sugar Grove schoolhouse; the "howdying" between old friends that met seldom and were glad to meet; the making of new acquaintances.

Then the volume of sound as each group in turn was called on and sang, swaying in time with the song, their hands waving in unison, so marking the rhythm with hand and body and voice.

Each set of contestants had brought its favorite hymn book. Sugar Grove was singing from "Windows of Heaven, No. 3," and most of the tunes were brand-new to all but these men, women, and children who had attended the singing school. The choir from Leaning Pine preferred their "Temperance Harp," in which new words were set to old tunes. To hear them sing: "Oh, what a good time that will be, when rum shall infest us no more," to an old camp meeting tune, was an experience.

Lonesome Creek took no prizes, nor looked for any, for the mighty singers of Lonesome had not been able to come, but the young people went home content, singing as they rode and tramped through the night, a night white with a full moon which lighted their way even through the thick woods.

Just before Christmas Lois closed her school with an exercise unequaled in the annals of Lonesome Creek, in which every last pupil took part in some way, and every parent had a chance to swell with pride. It was held in the afternoon that the mothers might come with the very little children, and the windows of the schoolhouse were darkened with quilts lent from a house near by, that the children might feel the occasion to be grand and gay. The school owned no lamps as yet, but lanterns were brought and hung on the walls so that by the time the house was "plumb full" there was light enough to manage with.

Shadrach made a short speech and Jim Wilder made a long one, but the gist of each was the same: that Middle-Lonesome wanted Miss Lois back again come August, and that next year a subscription could and would be made up to continue the school another month or two after "free money" was taught out.

It was harder for Lois to say goodbye to the Chalmers family than it had been to leave her own home sixteen weeks before. She laughed off her emotion by lamenting that she could not stay long enough to see the weaving of the linsey.

"Come back to us next year," said Martha, "and we'll sure fix it for you to stay longer. Then we'll be able to show you."

It fell out as they had wished and planned and for two more seasons and for longer sessions, Lois taught the school on the Creek. Then she would make no promises, but there was a secret conference with Martha before she set off in the wagon for the railroad and home.

Some time after this, Peaceable Tim's widow was visiting Granny Jude, whose cabin, far up a hollow, might be said to be the "top hen on the roost."

"Hev ye heard the news about Miss Lois?" said Granny. "They're a tellin' it that she's about to get married."

"It's plime-blank that-a-way," rejoined the other, "*and Martha's a-weavin' her weddin' dress.*"

4. THE THREE GRAY WOMEN

LOIS RICE was teaching for the second year the Middle-Lonesome School. It was fodder-pulling time and according to an ancient custom and by general consent the school was closed for a week. The children were in the fields, stripping off the lower leaves of the corn for "blade fodder" while the larger boys and the men were "topping" the stalks; cutting the "top fodder" with a quick, dexterous slash of the knife. Both kinds of fodder would make "roughness" on which the cattle would feed during the winter.

On Tuesday evening Esther Chalmers came to Lois with a message: "Maw wants you should go with her tomorrow to her aunts' in Tennessy. She's heard that Aunt Lizzie is kindly bad off, and she's took a notion to strike out and go over the mountain soon in the morning."

Lois accepted the summons gladly. Soon after sunrise she was on her way to the Chalmers to join Martha.

The night had been still, with a heavy frost, the first "killing frost" of the season. As Lois neared the big black walnut tree in the lane, where the children lingered after school to crack and eat the nuts, she saw that on the ground beneath it the leaves lay like a carpet, almost like a designed decoration; light, sharp green, toning up the brownish green grass and the brown earth around them. Above, the branches were almost bare. The flowers in the Chalmers yard, so gay the day before, were black, save for the chrysanthemums, bronze and yellow, that had withstood the cold.

Martha was ready and together she and Lois "took the mountain," thus cutting off many miles of travel by wagon road. At first they followed a logging road that wound in and out of the mountain side by easy grades. As they rounded an open slope, Lois saw a figure approaching them, in silhouette against the sky, tall and lank and sunbonneted.

"Yonder comes Serinthy Whissenbee," exclaimed Martha, "going to her brother's in the Holly Bottoms."

"How can she recognize a sunbonnet at this distance," thought Lois, to whom this headgear seemed a leveler and a disguise.

After greetings and polite inquiries after health, the two women sat down on a bank and engaged in the exchange of news. Lois watched with interest the movements of the two bonnets so close together, as they expressed the feelings of the speakers. She heard that Aunt Lizzie was on the mend though she had been "aiming to die."

"They plumb give her up," said Serinthy, "but Doc Burns come by and he fotched her out of it. They tell me he can cure mighty nigh anything that's a workin' on a body."

The mounting sun warned the wayfarers to be moving on so the last words were exchanged and Martha and Lois climbed on while Serinthy descended toward the Holly Bottoms with her budget of news.

When the crest of the mountain was gained, the travelers followed an obscure trail along a ridge and soon saw far below them Peachtree Cove, widening out into the flatwoods beyond, and far away they could dimly descry a town. Almost at their feet, in a fold of the hill above the Cove, lay the little homestead which was their goal.

A short descent through open woods and pasture brought them to the barns and to the house. There a scene of activity presented itself. What was being done was to Lois a mystery, no less so after Martha had exclaimed: "If they ain't right now a warpin' 'em a chain."

Against the house, a low structure of logs covered with weatherboarding, leaned a heavy wooden frame. On the ground in front of this stood a small upright frame, holding large spools filled with cotton yarn. Between the two moved an erect old woman, her hands filled with threads. These came from the spools and were being laid over and under pegs on the larger frame.

At the approach of the visitors, the warper, fastening her threads securely around a peg, stepped forward to greet her niece and then to make welcome the teacher. Aunt Elvira was the oldest of three sisters and Lois soon found that she had qualities lacking in the others. Her features, strong and rugged, were only relieved from ugliness by their expression. There was in her face not merely good will, but radiance that won Lois' heart.

Aunt Lizzie was sitting in a low "rocky chair," that had been brought out onto the grass before the house that she might watch "the doin's." She had a mouse-like face, with mouth drawn in, not only from loss of teeth, but from a shrewd suspicion of things in general and unwillingness to be committed to anything. Her neck was bound up with surgeon's plaster and she was not loath to tell how bad off she had been before Doc Burns had come.

"It warn't jest a plain risin', it war a kee-ar-bunkle," she explained with dignity. "I wor ne'er a one for much doctrine, but I mighty nigh faith Doc Burns."

Aunt Hannah was large, like her sister Elvira and like her was a master hand at the loom. Her specialty, a rare one, was the weaving of white counterpanes. The warp they were preparing was for her loom. Aunt Elvira, it was explained, wove coverlets, while Aunt Lizzie, when well, carded and spun and filled the quills for the others.

"They are like the Three Fates," thought Lois, "who spun and wove."

When Aunt Hannah began to tell her great trouble and would not cease telling it, about the loss of the one lens that had been left in her spectacles, without which she could not see to thread up her loom, and when she was joined in her lament by both of her sisters, Lois thought also of the Three Gray Women in the *Wonder Book,* who lost the one eye they had between them.

Still lamenting, Aunt Hannah set about getting dinner, while Aunt Elvira went on with the warping. Lois watched the process closely and with some explanation from Martha began to understand the method in what had looked to her quite aimless. The pegs had been set into the warping bars in a definite pattern. The purpose of the warping was to prepare a set of warp threads for winding upon the big back beam of the loom, so that they could be drawn forward, each thread in its own order, and each crossed with its neighbor threads. It is only so that the warp can be made to run smoothly and with even tension through the "gears," that is, the harness eyes, and through the reed to the front or cloth beam and be rolled on this as the web progresses. All this Lois comprehended but vaguely even when Elvira let her "pick the cross" at the end of a "bout," crossing each thread with the one next it and laying them all on the pegs so as to "hold the cross" until the warping was done and the crosses could be tied.

It was all interesting to Lois, but the prettiest sight came at the end, when Martha, tall and buxom, took the warp from the bars, looping the cream-white bunch of threads into itself, and laying this chain of great links over her shoulder as it lengthened. It was clear to anyone seeing this why the warp was, in common speech, the chain.

At the bountiful dinner the talk was all of the big meeting going on down in the settlement, four miles away.

"They do say it's the awfullest meetin' ever heard of. It's a regular tare-up of a meetin'," said Hannah, keen for excitement.

"Does seem like the people's takin' a interest," said Aunt Lizzie. "When the mourners get to takin' on and the others go to shoutin', you can't hear nothin'."

"Poor sister ain't fit to go anywheres till that neck of hers gets swaged down, but I'm aimin' to go and see for myself, come Sunday," said Hannah.

Aunt Elvira.

Aunt Hannah.

Warping the Chain.

Filling quills for the shuttle and
Carding.

Swifts, for winding
yarn.

"This poke-stalk religion ain't worth much, to my way of thinkin'," said Elvira, and seeing the puzzled look on Lois' face, she added, "Laws, child, ain't you seen pokeweed a growin' up so biggity in the summer time and then in winter, nothin' left of it but a gray rag you couldn't kinnle a fire with?"

Lois laughed as she recognized the aptness of the simile.

Early in the "evening" (a part of the day that begins at 12 M.), Martha prepared to start, for the days were shortening and she must be home by sundown. What was to be done about the missing lens? How could the web be drawn in? If Martha could stay, her eyes would suffice, but she had made no arrangement to be gone overnight. Timidly, Lois offered her services, and after some consultation it was decided that since she was a school-teacher she would be able to learn from Hannah to thread the harness. Outside of the help she might give, the three sisters were overjoyed to have the company for even one night and day of one they termed "a plumb sweet thing." Martha was uneasy at the thought of Lois "taking the mountain" alone the next day, fearing she might lose the trail, so blind in places. She bethought her that her "old man" was aiming to take his wheat around by road to the mill in the settlement below, and whenever he did so he could "come up by to fetch Miss Lois."

"Ef 'tain't tomorrow it'll be the next day."

So it was settled, and furthermore Shadrach could get a new pair of glasses at Bart's store on the way. "You can get them there," she said, "as low as ten cents."

This was most satisfactory, but Aunt Hannah gave one parting injunction for Shad to be "mighty perticklar to get specs, not glasses. Them that clinch the nose, I despise 'em."

Around the fire that evening there was comfort and good cheer. Lois told the three ancient dames about her home and her family in answer to their eager questions, and then heard from them of old times on the mountain; exciting tales of adventure with bear and wildcat and lynx; of deer hunts, of one when two of them as girls chased a stag over the mountains with their dogs a whole day and killed him at the Old Stand in North Carolina.

Then the subject of old songs came up; "love ballets," and ballad after ballad was sung. Elvira and Hannah had been famous singers in their day. "The False Knight upon the Road," "The Maid Freed from the Gallows," "The Silk Merchant's Daughter," "The Seven Bretheren," and others.

Some of them Lois had heard before, but others, centuries old, were new to her.

The last song, "Ellender and the Brown Girl," was sung alone by Hannah. She sat with head thrown back, eyes looking off as if she saw the things of which she sang acted out before her. Her voice, still strong and clear, intoned rather than sang the ancient tune with its gapped scale.

> Go dig my grave both wide and deep
> And paint my coffin black,
> And bury fair Ellender in my arms,
> The brown girl at my back.
>
> They dug his grave both wide and deep
> And painted his coffin black,
> They buried fair Ellender in his arms,
> The brown girl at his back.

At the end, Hannah said solemnly, "My mother taught me that and I *aim to not forget it*."

Lois woke early the next morning and taking a bucket ran to the spring for water over grass glistening with hoarfrost. A red dawn was in the eastern sky and high up, where the rose melted into gray-blue, a planet still shone. Looking toward the house she saw Elvira gazing at the beauty with her old face transfigured. "She sees it and feels it, too," said Lois softly.

Breakfast dispatched, the beaming of the web began. One end of the "chain" was fastened along the big beam and then laid over the "rake" whose teeth spread the threads apart. While one of the women turned the beam slowly, the others held the warp taut, paying it out as needed and watching that no thread caught in its progress. When all but a yard or two was thus rolled onto the big beam at the back of the loom, the ends of the threads were brought forward into position to be passed through the harness, a task requiring good eyesight.

Hannah went to a little chest under one of the beds and brought out the draft, rolled up and tied with black thread. When opened out, the long strip of yellowed paper showed a series of figures and crisscross lines in faded ink. Along the top was written: "Hannah McRae her County-Pin Draft." "A preacher drawed that off for me nigh on to fifty year ago," said Hannah. "Of all the county-pin drafts I've wove or seen wove, this is my favorite."

Lois felt horribly uncertain whether she could ever master the meaning of this mysterious paper, but her reputation as a teacher, and "high-larnt," was at stake, and make good she must. She took the place assigned her and listened intently to the instructions. There were before her four wooden frames, each holding many doubled threads, about eight inches long, and in the center of each pair was a loop or eye. The point was to get the right thread through the right eye. Hannah numbered the frames for her: one, two, three, and four.

"We'll commence with the selvedge," said she. "That ain't in the draft. You take these first two threads, here, and pass them through the first eye in the first harness. Yes, that's right. It'll go quicker once you've done it a spell. Now this next thread goes into the first eye in the second harness, the next 'un in the first on the third, and the next into that 'un on the fourth. Now one in the first harness, one in the second, and so on. It takes nine threads to make a plime-blank good edge for this kind of weaving. There's some that never learn that."

After the selvedge was successfully drawn in, they began with the draft. Lois soon found how this corresponded with the harness sets and harness eyes and the battle was won.

"I knew in reason she'd catch on to it," said Hannah, "but she's learnt the quickest ever."

"It takes more'n good sense," said Elvira, "she's been learned to put her thoughts on a thing and not let 'em squander all over creation."

Aunt Lizzie rocked to and fro in satisfaction, saying, "I just love to set and watch them pretty hands a flyin' about so spry. They're the *least* hands ever I see, on a woman."

With encouragement of this sort, Lois worked steadily and carefully at her self-imposed task. Though tiring, the novelty and importance of it kept it from becoming tiresome.

The last threads were drawn in by noon. As the four women sat down to dinner, Lois, weary but triumphant, heard the sound of wheels and the gee and haw of the mule driver. With the weird cry used in the mountains to stop the mules, Shadrach drew up before the house. After the "howdies" had been said the bridles were loosened and the bundles of "roughness" brought for the animals were thrown down before them. Shad, after a great splashing of hands and face in the basin on the porch rail, came in smiling benignly.

"He is always so joval," Aunt Hannah had said that morning, and jovial he looked with his clustering black locks and beard, as he opened his wallet and brought out, not one, but three pairs of spectacles of the desired sort.

The excitement though undemonstrative was intense, and the pleasure of each of the sisters as she found she could distinguish near objects with these new aids was good to witness.

In parting from Lois, both Aunt Hannah and Aunt Lizzie threw their old arms about her, "loving her neck," a sign of approval distinctly rare from them.

Elvira looked into her eyes and said, "I wish you well."

For Lois' comfort, Shad had brought on top of the load of wheat left at the mill, a splint-bottomed chair. On this, behind the driver's seat of rough board, she balanced herself in the moving wagon bed.

As the wheels half rolled, half slid down the steep road into the valley, she spoke thus with herself: "They are not one bit like Hawthorne's Gray Women except for the lost eye. His were quarrelsome and grasping, and these are generous and kind. Their religion isn't the poke-stalk kind. If ever I'm old and poor I want to be like Elvira. She *has something* I'll need then. I reckon I'd better begin to get it now."

5. COVERLETS

ANYONE to pass along through this country would think there warn't no one a livin' here much, but just let the people get up a interest in comin' out, and gin they swarm out of the hollows, they's a right smart crowd of them, git 'em all bunched up together."

So said a man of western North Carolina, and anyone who has lived for a season in the Carolina mountains can witness to the accuracy of his words. Adventuring off the main road and up one of the hollows, one comes to houses and cabins hidden away in the folds of the hills, not only from the stream of travel but for the most part from each other. To be "within hollerin' distance" of two or three other dwellings is to be in a center of population.

The approach to one of these farmsteads is known to a traveler on foot or in the saddle not only by the sight of the house with its cluster of out-buildings: barn, stable, corncrib, and smokehouse, but by the witness of the ear. A dog barks, or the guinea hens, holding a guinea-rights meeting on the Virginia rail fence, call stridently for rain; a woman is singing a child to sleep, and the sound of the chair in which she is rocking him to and fro, rockerless though it be, mingles with her high-pitched voice. It may be a "love ballet" she is singing, or one of the "songs of Zion." Or perhaps one hears the sound of children at happy play, or quarreling; in which case the mother is apt to be heard telling them to "quit their meanness," or she'll come out and "frail 'em with a stick."

From Granny Jude's cabin the sound most frequently heard was the dull thud of the loom batten, as the reeds of the sley struck in a regular rhythm, beating up the web. Granny Jude lived alone, for "that a way a body does see peace," but of casual visitors she could never have too many. To hear how the world about her wagged, and to pass on the news to the next comer, was the excitement of her life, as weaving was its occupation. Naturally her house was rarely without a neighbor woman who had "dropped in to sit a spell" to hear Town Topics, and to add, perchance, an item or an illuminating comment.

Gran, as she was called by those akin to her (and these included most of the people of the countryside), had had a varied experience. She had, so she said, "lived every way, hard and well enough, on the top of the pot and under it," and now again she was underneath. A fire had consumed her substantial house with most of its contents. Her savings, hidden between the square logs, had gone too. Living in the old cabin left to her, she was dependent on the product of her loom.

Life had, with her, been varied in other respects besides ease of circumstances. Her friends knew enough to refrain from awkward questioning. The virtues that were hers, of honest dealing and an open hand, gained her the respect and liking of the neighbors and they let bygones be bygones. As old man Chalmers sometimes said of the old days when Granny Jude was young: "There was no king in Israel, every man did that which was right in his own eyes."

When Granny Jude and Peaceable Tim's widow foregathered, there were stories recounted not only of the present doings on Lonesome Creek and its tributaries, but of old times during the war between the states, and even of still earlier times.

The little school-teacher, Lois Rice, liked to listen to those stories and they liked to have her for an audience. There were tales of the days when homes were three miles apart with only a trail between them; of the coming in of the first settlers, along the mountains from Pennsylvania; of the coming of "old man Chalmers of all," who lived with his family one whole winter in the hollow stump of an immense poplar tree. "They say he could swing a ten-foot pole in it." (Lois used to hope that the family was small and that the pole was not often swung about their heads.)

"Did you ever hear that by climbin' the Chestnut Knob, here at the top of the Creek, a body can walk to Pennsylvany without once crossin' water? There's them a livin' that's done it, in time of the war."

"Do you know how peoples did when the nearest mill was three days' journey off, and there weren't no neighbors? How the men-folks would go off once a year to the settlements to get their corn ground, packing it on mule-back or toting it their own selves?"

Once, when Gran's mother was left thus alone, a little feist trotted into the door at sundown, just such a little dog as was to be seen about every Indian encampment. Thinking that foes were upon her, the poor woman ran out of her house in terror and spent a long night crouching in the canebrake, but when she stole home in the dawn she found no sign of intruders.

"My mother was a powerful workin' woman," said Granny Jude. "She could do more weavin' in a day than I can in two, till along toward the last she was took with the deathly jerks or the deathly grab. It used to catch a holt of her at one side and go right acrost her. She sure was bad off.

"It was her taught me to weave coverlets. Used to when I was little I'd get into the loom when she was out and weave a piece of plain cloth. I never knowed if she noticed it, but one day she catched me at it. She gave me a genteel good breshing, but it caused her to let me learn coverlet weavin' like what I'm doing now. None of her other girls was turned that way. It's lucky I did learn it, for, as you may say, it's all my livin' these days, and it sure is hard to make a livin' out of plain weavin'."

"How many drafts is they?" in response to a question from the little teacher. "Laws a marcy, honey! That's something I can't tell ye. I can name them I've got and some I've seen wove, and some I've heerd tell of.

"That America, her that died a while back and they made such a pretty buryin' for, she'd take any coverlet that ever was wove, and, if she could get to ravel it out a bit, she'd set in and draw it in and tromp it same like she'd had a draft all writ out. She's the onliest one I ever did know that could do such as that.

"I don't know figures so I have to have marks, like on this draft pinned up on the loom. That's Pineburr, a mighty sweet draft. By now I know it so well that I can weave it right on without even flashin' my eye on the paper. Folks like this pattern so well I ain't scarcely no chance to try e'er a new one. I do delight in that. Delia, here, she brought me one from over the mountain called Philadelphia Pavement. I'm a rarin' to draw it in and see how the spots come out. Shucks, ain't it grand, the things they is to do and to find out about."

One day ill news came up the hollow to Granny Jude. Her son, the latest-born and the best-beloved, had been shot, just "yon side of the line." He had been the most to blame and had drawn his fate on him, but that did not lessen the blow to his mother. She sat with her apron over her head, bewailing her Joe, her "baby," or in ungovernable access of grief strode up and down before the cabin, leaping into the air, arms flung up, curses for the murderer on her lips.

Time quieted the ravings of her pain and new cares gave her less chance to brood. Joe's wife was a slim young thing "no bigger than a cake of soap after a week's washin'." Quite unfit to take up the battle of life for herself and the three "young-uns" clinging to her skirts. "Where is heart room there is hearth room," says an old proverb and Gran's heart and hearth were large enough for all. While the young widow cooked and washed and mended, Gran set herself resolutely to "beating out" on the loom the living for the five of them.

She thinks: "It's as near honor to work as anything that ever was done." No longer does she "see peace" in a quiet house to herself, but in the taking up of this heavy task in her old age, a higher and a better peace has come to her.

6. "HERB FOR THE SERVICE OF MAN"

WHILE she was in high school Lois Rice had studied botany, but with too little fieldwork to give her a real acquaintance with the plants of her region. The smattering she had learned of classification came back to her now when she was in the real country, and she became keenly interested in the flowering plants and the trees and shrubs on Lonesome. Armed with her Gray's *Manual,* she spent many leisure moments in identifying the specimens gathered from the roadside or brought to her by her pupils, who had grown interested in what they looked on as a new game of teacher's.

"You know the names, and we know the things," they said, as she named one of the plants so familiar to their eyes. One evening in November, as Lois reached the Poplar Gap on her way home from school, she heard in the woods above the road the sound of chopping; but not the sharp, decisive stroke of the woodsman. Looking up she saw her hostess, Mrs. Jim Wilder, at work with a hatchet at the roots of a large tree.

Lois felt for Mrs. Jim both liking and respect. In looks she was far from the type usually described in mountain fiction. Of medium height, she had put on flesh with the years. In spite of weight that made her unwieldy and her gait a roll rather than a walk, she was on her feet and in motion most of the time from before dawn to after dark. A woman of executive gifts, she turned off the work of the house with seeming ease, and looked also after the varied interests of her husband during his frequent absences on business. Her many children were taught early to look out for themselves and for each other, and though it could not be said that they were tidy, their rosy faces and stoutness of limb showed them to have suffered nothing from their mother's seeming neglect.

All but the youngest of the flock were boys, and to supply the place of older daughters, Mrs. Jim had adopted two orphan girls, who fared well with the others.

Seeing Lois in the road below her, Mrs. Jim called to her and Lois ran up the steep bank, eager to see what her hostess was doing so out of her common round.

"I'm huntin' me some white walnut roots to dye yarn for the boys' jeans," said Mrs. Jim. "A body might think that with all them boys of mine I'd not have to do such as this, but they're mighty trifling and fergetful when it comes to anythin' they 'low is work for weemin. I'd full as soon do it myself as to be quarrelin' at 'em about it.

"What will these roots make? The purtiest sort of a black, for a black and white mixtry. I'll be needin' some sumac berries, too, but they grow down the road a piece."

As the two walked along together toward home, Lois thought to herself that here was another piece of the puzzle that excited her interest: the coloring of the homespun cloth. She had not taken much thought about that part before. How were the other colors obtained? Did they, too, come from the woods, she wondered?

It was easy, she learned from Mrs. Jim, to get all shades of yellow and orange and brown. "For red, there ain't one thing in the woods that grows here, wild, to make you a right, bright red. Mam has madder in her garden and that is a fine color if a body knows how to work with it. Mam is the masterishest body in this settlement for all kinds of coloring. You'd oughter talk to her. She's been setting a blue pot here lately."

The suggestion was not lost on Lois. Peaceable Tim's widow had often begged her to spend the day with her, and why not go up next Saturday with Ursula, the youngest of the Wilder flock.

Lois' mind was well imbued with the maxim: a teacher should have no favorites. In the schoolroom she managed to keep an impartial rule. Her feelings, however, could not be so easily controlled. Between her and seven-year-old Ursula there was a bond of understanding and affection that grew stronger with the weeks. The child was small for her age but with limbs well rounded. Every motion was full of unconscious grace, the result of perfect health and of her buoyant spirit. Her comrades, both boy and girl, acknowledged her charm without realizing it, but when John Wesley, a red-headed urchin, gave expression to his liking one recess time, by confronting her with: "Me and you stand in, don't we, Urse?" she gave his cheek a resounding slap and danced away to the other side of the playground, leaving him to gaze ruefully after her.

It was not for her winning looks and ways alone that Lois loved the child, but most for an inner quality. From the day when they found out that each felt what Lois called "quivery" over the wild flowers and mosses and ferns that lined the roadways and hid in the woods, the two understood each other. Ursula had found a friend to whom she could talk out the thoughts her busy mother could not listen nor respond to, and Lois, in the child's freshness and beauty of spirit, found renewal of the child's heart in herself.

A last word.　　　　　　　　Her own work.

The Dye Pot.

R. S. W.

Home from school.

So on Saturday morning, taking the road up the hollow to the Walnut Flats, the two talked of many things in earth and heaven to their great satisfaction.

Arrived at her grandmother's, Ursula looked in at the door, and, seeing her grandmother busied by the fire, ran out to her "playhouse" at the edge of the woods, where on a background of mosses were displayed various treasures: bits of colored china and of glassware, a toy whittled out by one of her brothers, a shiny piece of tin.

As Lois went into the cabin, the widow of Peaceable Tim was bending over an enormous black iron pot, dipping up its liquid contents in a tin cup and letting them fall back into the pot. As Lois drew near the fireplace, the old woman straightened up and said, "Git you a cheer and rest you up a spell after climbin' this mountain.

"You-all ain't as used to it as I be," she continued, after a pause filled with constant dipping. "For forty years I've ben a travelin' up and down this road, as long as the children of Israel were a travelin' up and down through the wilderness.

"I sort of suspicioned you'n Ursie might be a travelin' it today, being as it's Saturday and sech a perty day. Where *is* the child? I reckon she come with ye?"

"She's out looking after her pretties," replied Lois. "But is this the blue pot? Why does it foam so and why is it *green*? I should think it would be *blue*."

The old woman smiled as she said, "Hit's green, and hit colors blue. It sure looks quare to a body, but 'tis so."

"But what is in the pot? And why are you dipping it up that way?"

"It's just now *come*, and I'm gettin' the air into it.

"What's in it? says you; there's indigo in it; a leetle mite of a ounce or two, squeezed through a little cloth sack, and the same of madder. But mind ye, the madder has to be fresh or it does no good. It's quick to lose strenth. That in there come from my own garden and it's a heap stronger than that you can buy at the store.

"Then there's bran (it has to be wheat bran); and lye. Some has trouble colorin' blue on account of not havin' real old-fashioned lye, dripped from hardwood ashes, that ha' ben burnt over and over in the fireplace."

"Do you put the ashes right in with the other things?"

"Bless you, no, honey! The ashes goes into that ash hopper out in the yard. The rain washes down through 'em and leaches 'em, and the lye drips out at the small eend of the hopper. It's the lye that goes into the pot. Then you fill up the pot with water just warm to your hand and let it set, where it'll keep about so warm. I keep the seed of my fire all night, so the corner here is warm a plenty for the pot."

"How long do you have to wait for it to be ready to dye with?" said Lois.

"Times it comes in a week or such a matter; times a body has to wait on it longer. It jest comes whenever it gits ready. You can tell when it comes by the greeny look in the foam. Then you take and dip it a while like I'm a doin' and then let it set a day or two more till it's good and foamy. After that you can go to dippin' the yarn.

"How's that done? First you put a plate in bottom side up to keep the bran from risin' and gettin' all mixed in with the wool. Then you dip in your lot of wool or your yarn and hang it up out of doors and in a little while you dip it in agin and you keep on a doin' of it that-a-way till the color's as deep as you want it. For pale blue I ginerally has to dip four or five times and more for right deep blue."

"Dear me!" exclaimed Lois, "there's plenty of work about it!"

"I'll not say it's not a worrisome job, but if a body's turned that way, like I am, there's a heap of satisfaction in it."

"Your daughter says you make red with madder. Do you set a pot like this?"

"It's kindly like it but it's easier done and sooner over with. Jest madder and bran and water, and when it sours good it's ready. Some puts in vinegar, but I kin do without. I'll show you the prettiest madder color ever you see," and turning down the white sheet spread over the bed in the corner farthest from the fireplace, the company bed, the old woman displayed a coverlet in red and white, beautiful and rich in color.

"That was dyed and spun and wove by a sister of my old man's. It's called 'Missouri Trouble.' Reckon there *was* trouble in Missouri way back yonder in them days."

After this visit, Lois still pursued her investigations anent dye plants. She plucked and triumphantly analyzed the "dye flower," a species of coreopsis, found high up on the mountain ridges. Later she helped to gather the "bay leaves."

She made note of the fact that "sneezeweed" makes a pretty yellow, but not fast color, and that broom sedge gives a different hue for almost every month of the year.

In January measles appeared in the school. No quarantine could be maintained and the disease, very light in the first cases, spread rapidly. When Ursula's turn came, however, it went hard with her; the usual herb teas had little effect in bringing out the eruption.

Mrs. Jim, with her everyday, shrewd, business expression replaced by one of anxious and tender love, held the child in her arms, rocking her, and murmuring pet names in her ear. Ursula lay unresponsive, her cheeks bright red, every breath a struggle.

"She's sure taken the fever," was the dictum of her grandmother.

"Couldn't you send for that Dr. Burns I've heard so much about?" ventured Lois. But no, "Doc Burns" had been about them only during vacations when he was studying; now he was established in a large town far away.

"If even old Doc Sutton was living, him we always called 'Old Redbeard,' he was a good man and a kind one, but he's gone," said Jim. " 'Pears like we're kindly bad off for doctrine."

As a last resort, one of the boys was sent off to Ellsworth to see if a doctor could be found there willing to come. Lois, who shared the mother's watch that night, will never forget the slow passing of the hours, the ticking of the clock, and at last, at one in the morning, the barking of the dogs down the creek, warning them that someone was on the road, and then the hoof-falls of one horse, bringing back the messenger alone. No help could be looked for from Ellsworth.

Lois, desperate, summoned her energies and searched her memory. "Is there any mustard in the house?" she asked Mrs. Jim.

Ground mustard there was none, but there must be mustard seed in one of the small gourds hanging in the kitchen porch, and holding the seeds for the garden. After a frantic search the seeds were discovered. Lois poured them into a wooden bowl, and, running out into the yard, picked up a smooth rock for a pestle.

With only half a hope to sustain her sinking heart, she mashed the seed, mixed them with water, and spread the paste on one of her handkerchiefs. Then, laying the plaster on Ursula's breast, she with the mother hung over the child, in suspense.

It was not long before the labored breathing seemed to their anxious watch to be slightly eased. In half an hour they were assured that the improvement was not imagined but real, and together they wept from sheer relief and joy.

When the scourge was over, school reassembled, and Ursula quite herself again, her grandmother, settled for the day by Jim's fireside, reviewed the events just past and delivered her oracle.

"There's something a growin' in the fields or in the woods, if folks only knowed what they are, that'll cure most every complaint there is. There's boneset, and wintergreen, and angelica, and snakeroot, and a power of other yarbs, not to tell of this here mustard that holp us out with little Urse. I reckon the Lord that made 'em planned it out that-a-way for our good."

7. WORK OF THE WISE-HEARTED

JIM WILDER hitched his chair around from the table and tilting back in it was ready for conversation.

"I see Aunt Cinthy Duncan over to Rocky Lonesome," said he, "her and her leetle old wagon and the brown mares. She's stoppin' over to Jake Simmonses. We'll maybe see her here next week."

Mrs. Jim, having already seen to it that her household was fed, poured herself a cup of coffee from the big pot on the cookstove, and settled herself to listen and ask questions.

"How'd she say she was?" said she.

"Like she allays is, sorter poky, and on the backgrounds, but she 'peared to be mighty peart for the age she's gettin' to be. She must be upwards in sixty."

Lois had before this heard something of Aunt Cinthy and had gathered that she was a personage. Her visits to Lonesome and the adjacent regions, made at irregular intervals, and extending over several weeks, were regarded by her kinsfolk in the light of semiroyal progresses. In the ten days that elapsed between Jim's announcement and the arrival of the great lady, Lois learned much more about her.

"She was raised right nigh to Middle-Lonesome," Mrs. Jim told her. "You recollect that big log house up the Piney Fork on Matt Corvin's place behind the house he lives in now? It's kindly tore down now, but it was a pretty good dwellin' in its day and time. Cinthy's maw was a Chalmers, sister to Shad's paw. Her boys was all gals and the whole passel of 'em was put to making the crop as soon as they was big enough to hannel a hoe. Cinthy's pap did the plowing, he said it looked the awkwardest to him to see a woman a plowing. Sometimes he'd harrow. The gals did the rest. Cinthy, she delighted in it, she hated to be tied to the house, she was a master hand for field work."

"What did the father do, if the girls did all the work?"

"You say, what did he do? He hunted some, but most days he just loafered round. He was mighty public-spirited, always ready to stop and set on a fence and talk politics or any of them other things men-folks go on about when there's three or four of 'em together. He certainly could consume the day with such as that.

"The main trouble though was the way he had of gambling. He was sure born a gambler. That's what kept his family on suffrance. They made 'em plenty, but he'd lose it all at his little card games. I've heard my father tell about him losing their cow one time. The gals had made a pet of her and they all run off and hid, so's not to see her go; all but Cinthy. She was crying but she was mad, too, clear through. She stood there a stampin' her foot and cussin'. Them was hard times for the pore gal, but she sure done well for herself when she married Dick Duncan."

At another time Lois heard more about this rich marriage. Dick Duncan was a trader in horses and mules, well known throughout the country.

"He'd come through here a buying 'em up, and he'd take whole strings of 'em back to Tennessy. Used to when we was little, we'd make us horses out of cornstalks. You've seen them little tricks? I reckon the children make 'em yet. We'd call ours Duncan's horses and we'd play at selling 'em to him.

"Cinthy was a likely gal; her hair was all black and curly, like Shad's gal, Millie, and her eyes had a snap to 'em. Duncan see her when he'd trade with her pap, and first thing anyone knowed they was married. I see them go off together and me a little kid. He'd brought her a fine sidesaddle and she was riding along careless like, same like a man (she was ne'er a mite afeerd of a critter) and her eyes were a sparkling.

"Duncan was a good man to her, she had plenty while he lived, and he made her a free woman before that, so she controls everything."

In due time Aunt Cinthy reached Middle-Lonesome. Her first stop was at Jim Wilder's, where she shared Lois' room. The two had full opportunity to become acquainted. From the first Aunt Cinthy approved of the girl.

"She's not one mite like the foolish young things out where I live. All they can think of is to get into town where they can see something. I can see plenty to suit me in the country. That's one thing I like about Miss Lois, here, she takes note of what's about her."

Though "upwards, and well upwards in sixty," Mrs. Duncan's hair was still black and her eyes had not lost their snap. She was of large frame and well formed. Her movements indicated health and vigor. There was an air of out of doors about her that acted like a tonic.

Aunt Cinthy soon discovered Lois' interest not only in the things in the country, but in the old-time ways of living.

"Ain't it a refreshment to the spirit, as the preachers say, to see any young person that takes a real hearty interest in them old coverlets and work such as that?" she said one day. "And you, that has been somewhere and has got book learning, to set a high value to these old things! I love 'em myself, though I'd rather be switched anytime than try to make 'em. I ain't turned that way. But them little old fixin's of young weemen that live about me on the River they ain't got no use for them coverlets and county-pins and teesters; make fun of them; they do so. I'm plain tired of them; them and their powders and their goings on. They rub their cheeks with them artificials, to make 'em red. Better get out, I says to them, and hoe 'em a row or two and they'd have color enough to last 'em a spell. They ain't no idea of work nor the worth of work in *the* world. One of my daughter-in-laws is like that. 'I am weary of my life because of the daughters of Heth,' as the Good Book says."

Mrs. Duncan on leaving the Wilders begged Lois to come down to spend a week with her at Christmas time, promising to show her specimens of handwork. "My house is mighty nigh filled with it, what-all came from his folks is there, mighty nigh all of it, they tell me, and there's some from the Chalmers side and from my pap's people, so you'll see something, I'm a telling you.

"Come about Christmas time; you give these pore young-uns a holiday, don't ye? I'll send the hack for you. Jake Byron can drive the mules. He's a candidate for mattimony too, but don't you take up with him; he's too old for a pretty young thing like you."

At first Lois demurred on account of the expected visit from her sister Susan during the holidays, but the invitation was extended to Susan also, and urged so heartily that Lois accepted it with genuine pleasure.

On the day set Byron appeared with the well-known outfit from the Duncan place. The road at first was familiar to Lois but when the turn was made through the Hollow Gap, all was new to her. A light snow had fallen and had melted off around Middle-Lonesome, but up on the mountain it still lay, throwing into relief the laurels and the leafless scrub. The sun in a sky of bright blue warmed the travelers and the mules took them along at a smart pace.

Descending on the other side of the Gap the character of the country changed. Though still broken, it became less rugged, the fields were larger and more level. To a farmer's eye it was a more attractive land. For the two young women, however, it lacked the charm of the wilder country.

It was late in the day when they approached the River and saw before them wide fields, and large barns and a house of good proportions. "Is that the Duncan place?" cried the girls.

"That's what we call it," said Byron, "I 'lowed you-all couldn't misunderstand it."

It was a good farm, well kept up. The chimneys smoked in welcome and soon Mrs. Duncan was bringing in her guests and making much of them. With her lived a cousin of her husband, whom she called Cousin Mag. On her, it would seem, devolved the management of the household, leaving Mrs. Duncan free to devote herself to the affairs of the farm; an arrangement that made for peace and comfort.

The exhibition of handwork began that night. The supper table was spread with a fair linen cloth, woven a hundred years before. It was white and shining after its many launderings. "It's wove in 'Rings and Chains,'" Cousin Mag told them. "Some of them's in 'M's and O's,' but I always did like 'Rings and Chains' the best. The flax was raised and worked by my Great-grandmother Duncan, down about Raleigh. She was born in the old country and come across in a sloop after one of them leetle rebellions they had over there in Ireland. Her folks was into it and they had to flee."

The night was cold but in the large room into which the girls were ushered at bedtime a wood fire was burning in the big chimney place, giving light as well as heat. The covers on the bed were many and some of the names of the patterns were mentioned by Cousin Mag as she turned them down for the sleepy girls. They laid their heads on the pillows with a confused sense of being beneath a battlefield where Bonaparte's men were marching to the Defeat of Braddock. They knew nothing more until the morning sun of December came through the pure white window curtains and Cousin Mag came in with a handmaiden to lay their fire.

It had "put in a pretty good night's rain," as Aunt Cinthy said, and the leaves of the evergreen shrubs around the house that had curled up tightly in the severe cold were smoothed out and glistening in the sunlight.

Aunt Cinthy said of the rain, "All we get now we won't be bothered with next spring when we're wanting some spring weather."

The days spent at the Duncan farm did not lack interest. The girls spent their mornings in the open air, with Mrs. Duncan or alone, going over the farm, walking through woods and fields. In the afternoons the treasures from wardrobes and shelves and drawers were brought out for their admiration.

The coverlets were many, of various designs and of various colors, though the deep indigo blue held the first place. A bright scarlet cover was colored by a great-aunt, so Cousin Mag said, with "Scotch chenille." But this was a rarity among coverlets and had an exotic look that did not please Lois like the softer reds and browns. She liked to trace the evolution of the patterns. "St. Ann's Robe," for instance, became "Governor's Garden," and then with a change in proportions, "Pokendalis." What that name meant puzzled her and she repeated it over wonderingly, till Susan, whose favorite study was history, exclaimed, "Pokendalis, Pokendallis. I believe it is Polk and Dallas! I was reading the other day about Dallas, Texas, being named for the Vice-President with Polk." This was greeted by the old ladies as a great discovery, and the draft of the coverlet was hunted up that the name might be written in its corrected form.

"All the same," said Lois, "I like Pokendalis better. It sounds like something in a fairy tale."

Susan was interested in the Old World names such as "Irish Chain," "Flowers of Edinboro," "Germany's Star." Lois, the flower lover, liked the "Dogwood Blossom" and the "Hickory Leaf."

Though the counterpanes did not bear such piquant names, being mostly variants of "dimities" and "huckabuck stripe," they were very lovely with their cream-white surfaces and with their elaborate fringes. There were testers, too; and some of these of netted work and fringe were in use on the high-post beds. A set of window curtains with borders of drawn work had been laid away carefully in a chest.

"Them was made by my Grandmother Chalmers," said Mrs. Duncan. "She was a master hand at weavin' and all kinds of such-like. This here," indicating the needlework, "was all done in the loom. Them spaces was never made by drawing out the threads, like you see people a doing in these days; she jest bowdaciously *left out* the threads whenever she wanted to work it this-a-way."

When they came to the quilts, Cousin Mag was in her element.

"I do naterally love a scrop quilt," she said. "Time was I could piece you any quilt you could name, from a 'Blazin' Star' to the 'Ocean Wave.'"

"You're a wonderin' why I cain't do it now. It's on account of me havin' the neuralgy so bad and whenever I go to workin' with the needle it makes it worser. It's jest a continual, severe misery!"

There were piece quilts enough to furnish forth two large families. Many of these were "scrop quilts," made out of bits of the family dresses, and of odds and ends of all sorts.

"Somethin' out of nothin'," Cousin Mag called them.

A few were made out of whole cloth. "The Road to California and Back" was in red and green and white; "The Sunflower," gorgeous in green and orange and white.

The "Patchwork" spreads (*appliqué*) were rare, but there were one or two admirable specimens, well preserved, and elaborately quilted.

"The woman that made that had lots of sense or she couldn't have quilted it up that-a-way," was Aunt Cinthy's comment on the handsomest of all.

There was one of plainer design, the "Bear's Paw," that had seen hard usage. Aunt Cinthy explained that this was her mother's work.

"She was allays a workin' at suthin' and I recollect when she was at this. Paw had had good luck one time and he brought us a dress pattern apiece from town. Maw she cut these Bear's Paws outen the scraps and patched 'em onto this old flax sheet that was made in past generations.

"You'll see some of the pieces is red and some is brown and some is yaller and some is green, jest like our dresses was. I can pick 'em out now. That there red 'un is mine. Folks knowed in them days what bears' paws was like, without visitin' a show to find out."

Laid away in the chest where were stored the chief treasures of the collection was a spread that showed the initiative of Grandmother Chalmers: a homespun sheet on which she had embroidered a pattern of her own designing in chain stitch and overlaid work. The thread used, homespun cotton, had been colored with indigo and with turkey red. The effect was charming. Grandmother Chalmers had made three of these spreads, one for each of her daughters.

"Two were alike," said Aunt Cinthy, "and one different. That un has zigzags all acrost it like Virginny rail fences. Polly Ann Frobisher has that un; she lives over on Piney. Her maw was sister to my maw. I reckon Aunt Delia has the mate to this un, if she hain't give it to Jim Wilder's wife. You hain't seen it? I reckon they never once thought of bringin' it out."

Among the blankets were one or two pieces of all wool material, of intricate design, the only specimens of weaving in which a wool warp had been used. Cousin Mag displayed with pride a "breakfast shawl," a triangle for the shoulders, all wool, but not woven on a loom. It was made of strands of wool, which had been fastened in a wooden frame and tied together closely enough to make a warm fabric.

Last of all came the tufted and the knotted spreads, which were wholly new to Lois. She and Susan were curious to find out how the tufting was done, and it was not until Cousin Mag had explained how the candlewicking was drawn through the cloth with a thick needle and then clipped between the stitches, that their minds were free to admire the spreads and to distinguish the patterns. The most interesting was one worked in close tufts on a homespun cotton sheet.

"My grandmaw worked that," Cousin Mag told them. "She made up the pattern as she went along. I've heerd my maw tell how Gran'd set and study about it and then she'd slip out into the dooryard and pick her some pretties and work 'em in. Them's Marigolds and these here is Prince's-feather, some calls 'em Cockscombs. Do you take note of that leetle baby hand worked in the corner? That's my aunt's hand. Gran jest had her to hold it there and she marked around it and then worked it in.

"I wouldn't sell it for all the gold of the Queen of Sheby, but I copied it once, all but that leetle hand. It was for a woman who came in here once from way off yonder some'ers. It give me a stiddy job, working at it dodge times for three months. She paid me well for it, give me twenty dollars; wanted it for her son's wife, she said. A mighty fine woman."

Most of the spreads had names such as "Bird in the Tree," "Bowl of Roses," "Cucumber Vine," and "Wild Rose Vine." A more formal pattern was named "Napoleon's Wreath."

Lois and Susan contended playfully as to the merits of the two kinds of work, Susan preferring the newer knotted spreads where the pattern was outlined in French knots made of the threads of the candlewicking. Lois held to her first liking for the "turfed" work.

"It is so much more grandmotherish," she said.

The last day of their visit was Sunday, the first Sunday of the month and of the year. There was to be preaching that morning in a church house not far away.

"Christians is mighty scatterin' around here," said Aunt Cinthy, "but ther'll be several out to hear Elder Ryan."

"It does me good just to see Elder Ryan," said Cousin Mag. "He is so antic and talks vigorous."

"Laws a marcy! Mag! That ain't no reason for likin' him," rejoined Cinthy, "but he sure is a good speaker. He can stand up there and the preach comes out of him. He hits the truth every time and it hits you. And he don't spend no time in no denominational denominalities."

The four women, and Jake Byron with them, walked to the church house built on rising ground. Other little parties on foot were on the road and now and then a wagon passed, its occupants sitting on splint-bottomed chairs that filled the wagon bed. There were many riders on mule or horse. The "appointment" was for ten o'clock, but as someone remarked, "He always gives the people plenty of time, and it'll likely be eleven when he begins." The women entered the church and seated themselves on the left side. Most of the men and boys stood on the porch or in groups in the yard, in subdued conversation.

When the preacher rode up on his sturdy bay horse, Lois could see him through the window as he swung from the saddle and fastened his mount to a young oak tree. Saddlebags on his arm, he stood for a few moments, "howdying" one and another and then entered the house. Calling some of the singers up to the seats near the desk, he started a hymn. The first line was sung as a solo, the singers swinging in on the second. The sound brought the men into the building and hastened the steps of the late comers up the hill; a hill hard to climb in haste with its slippery clay and dead leaves.

The service was hearty. The sermon was one that went to the hearts of most of the hearers, certainly to the hearts of Lois and Susan.

Jake Byron spoke for himself and possibly for other hearers when he joined the party outside of the church house: "That was a powerful serment, I jest set thar a thinkin' and a thinkin' how good it was fer Bill Saunders."

Elder Ryan was taking dinner at the Duncan house that noon before going on to another appointment. He was a hale old man in his seventies, white haired and ruddy of countenance from continued exposure to the weather. His younger days had been passed as a frontier circuit rider where he had borne hardship and had learned in frontier life the best and the worst of human nature; growing ever in good will as he grew in wisdom.

Table talk when he was present was cheerful and often merry. On this occasion it turned after a while to the old-time works and ways, and to the interest in these felt by the two young people. Lois being questioned by the Elder said: "I can't give a reason for my feelings about those things the women worked at in the old days; it wasn't religion, like preaching and converting people, and yet it seems almost religious to me."

The Elder looked at her quizzically and with understanding. "A good many people have the idea that the Spirit of the Lord has to do only with preachers or with other people when they are saying their prayers," he remarked. "Give me the Good Book." Finding his place he read: "And the Lord spake unto Moses, saying, See I have called by name Bezaleel the son of Uri, the son of Hur, of the tribe of Judah; and I have filled him with the Spirit of God in wisdom and in understanding and in knowledge, and in all manner of *workmanship*."

"There is a young fellow in our circuit; I meet him often in Conference, a mighty fine man; a good preacher and a good liver. He's always quoting out of a little book by R. L. Stevenson, he calls it the 'gospel according to Robert Louis.' It seems to me like a piece of the old Gospel. Here's a part of it I got him to write out for me."

Taking a wallet from his pocket, the old man turned over the papers till he found what he wanted, a thin slip of paper, and read from it:

> For still the Lord is Lord of Might;
> In deeds, in deeds, he takes delight;
> The plough, the spear, the laden barks,
> The field, the founded city, marks;
> He marks the smiler of the streets,
> The singer upon garden seats;
> He sees the climber in the rocks;
> To him the shepherd folds his flocks.
> For those he loves that underprop
> With daily virtues heaven's top,
> And bear the falling skies with ease,
> Unfrowning caryatides.
> Those he approves that ply the trade,
> That rock the child, that wed the maid,
> That with weak virtues, weaker hands,
> Sow gladness on the peopled lands,
> And still with laughter, song and shout,
> Spin the great wheel of earth about.

"It helps, doesn't it," said Lois with shining eyes, "to know that God cares how work is done!"

"Yes, it helps," said the old man slowly, "to know that our Maker trusts us that way. You, Mrs. Duncan, with your gift for animals; you, Miss Margaret, with your domestical duties, like those women who wrought well and honestly in the old time, scorning to leave a bauchle in their work; Miss Lois and Miss Susan with their books and their teaching; Jake, here, with his strength leaving ne'er a crooked furrow behind him and never ill to the stock; I with my circuit; we are called to do the work of the world."

"I'll be doggoned ef he ain't preached us a sarment I have obleeged to take to myself," said Jake, under his breath.

APPENDIX I

THE WORKING OF THE LOOM

THE "gears" or "harnesses" are designed solely to open the sheds. A harness set (called in a power loom a heddle-frame) is a frame about forty inches long and some twelve or fifteen inches high, hung about midway between the back and breast beams and parallel with these and athwart the warp threads. Along this frame are strung from top to bottom the harness eyes, double threads each with a loop in the center, the eye, through which passes one of the warp threads. In plain weaving two harness sets only are needed, which are hung by strings and leather straps over a crossbar at the top of the loom, and so face the weaver when she takes her seat on the bench in front of the breast beam. Each harness set is attached at the bottom by a cord to a treadle working on a crossbar near the floor. When the weaver "tromps" on one of these treadles the harness to which it is tied is lowered while the other harness goes up; threads 1, 3, 5, and so on are depressed, and the alternate threads, passing them, are raised. Between them is left an open space, the shed, for the passage of the shuttle from one side to the other. The foot is held firmly on the treadle until the shuttle has been thrown, then it is loosened and the weaver swings the batten toward her with a good strong "lick" and the second "lick" is more effective if she has meanwhile "tromped" the other treadle and so opened the other shed for the shuttle's return.

The batten is in front of the harness and the shuttle passes directly in front of it. This is a wooden frame in which the sley is firmly clamped and is swung from the top bars of the loom or moves back and forth on rockers at the bottom of the loom frame. The sley is in reality a comb with the teeth held on either end in a light wooden frame. Its teeth were in the old days made of reed or river cane, but there are few sley makers left now who can set the teeth evenly, and factory-made reeds have teeth of steel. When the shed is opened the place for the batten is back against the harnesses so that the shuttle can fly across in front of it. After the passing of each thread of woof through its shed the batten is brought forward with a quick, sharp stroke, "one lick for blankets," "two for linsey."

It is in order to make it easier to keep the threads in order and untangled as they run out their forty or fifty yards from the big beam, and to assist the weaver in knowing what thread should come next, as she passes the warp threads through the harness eyes, that the "warping bars" do their work. This process of warping has been already described, but will perhaps be better understood when taken in connection with the description of the work of the harnesses. The threads for a warp are wound upon large spools and from these are laid upon and around certain pegs in a frame, the

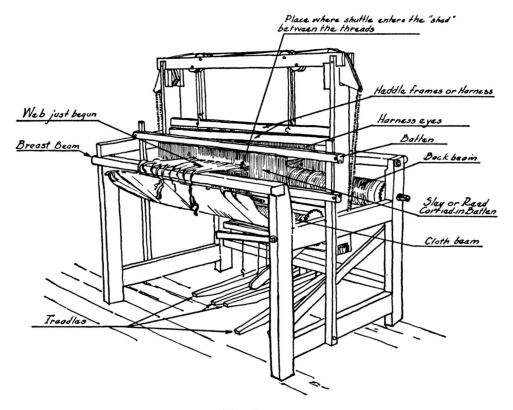

Place where shuttle enters the "shed" between the threads

Haddle frames or Harness

Harness eyes

Batten

Back beam

Web just begun

Breast Beam

Slay or Reed Carried in Batten

Cloth beam

Treadles

The Loom.

warping bars. This separates the two sets of threads which are thus left crossing each other. Before the warp (or chain) is taken from the bars these "crosses" are tied in several places. As the warp is being "beamed," that is, rolled onto the big beam of the loom, it is spread out to the proper width by being laid between the teeth of the rake. The rake is not attached to the loom and is only used while beaming the warp. It keeps the warp spread out so that it winds evenly on the beam and without tangling. Smooth rods are slipped in where the "crosses" were tied, so that the two sets of threads are on separate sides of each rod. These rods holding the "cross" are left behind the harness between them and the big beam, and as the web progresses the warp threads pass on over them. In a picture of a Grecian loom of long ago may be seen the sticks or rods holding the cross.

When the beaming is done, the whole of the warp has been wound upon the back beam except for the last yard or two in which are the important rods. The worker takes her seat at the side of the loom, opposite or a little back of the harness, and begins to pass the ends of the warp threads forward and through the harness eyes. After a few have been put in double to make a firm selvedge, she begins with what we have called thread No. 1. This she puts through the first harness eye in back harness set and thread No. 2 is passed through the first eye in the front harness. No. 3 goes into the second eye in the back harness and No. 4 into the second eye in front harness, and so on across the web until there are just enough threads to make the selvedge on the farther side. By means of the cross rods she has no difficulty in knowing which thread comes next.

To draw in thus a web of the usual width, 36 or 38 inches, two workers are needed, one to pass the threads through from the back and the other, sitting in front, to receive and hold them till they are secured in some way.

After the threads are all through the harness, comes the task of passing each thread through the sley. For a firm cloth two threads go into each slit between the sley teeth, but they must be the right threads coming in order.

The ends, once drawn through the harness and sley, are passed over the breast beam and tied or otherwise fastened to the cloth beam and both back and cloth beams are turned till the web is taut and are then caught and held by little iron "dogs" that fall into cogs at the right-hand end of each beam.

In what is known as "coverlet weaving" or "overshot weaving," a pattern or "draft" is necessary.

A draft, as we have seen, is not needed for plain weaving, but if one were made it might read thus:

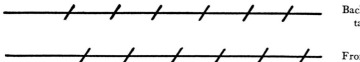

Back harness and treadle attached to it

Front harness and its treadle

Where three harness sets are used as in the weaving of jeans the draft might run thus:

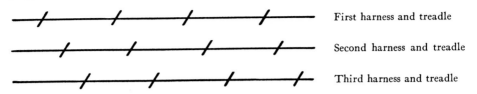

First harness and treadle

Second harness and treadle

Third harness and treadle

In these drafts the long lines represent the harness in drawing in the warp threads and the treadles in tramping for opening threads. The dashes across the long lines represent the warp threads, showing in what order they are to be passed through the harness eyes, or rather, in which harness set each thread belongs. The tramping follows the same rule; each dash representing a warp thread in drawing in, represents in tramping also the order in which the treadles are tramped.

When we come to coverlet weaving the drawing in through the harness and the treadle work, "tromping," is more complicated but still not hard to grasp. There is a groundwork of plain weaving on which (or shot over it) appears the design. In the usual coverlet the warp is of white cotton and the woof threads which make the plain cloth under and through the design are also of white cotton and called "binders." The woof threads that make the pattern are of wool yarn colored.

Four sets of harness are necessary. With the warp threads distributed on these four sets it is possible by tramping two treadles together to open, not two sheds only as in plain weaving but six different sheds. Two of these give the sheds for plain cloth, where every other warp thread is raised and the alternate threads depressed, and *vice versa*. The other four sheds are for the passage of the colored yarn in making the pattern.

The six sheds are thus opened:

    1. Tramp treadles 1 and 2
    2. Tramp treadles 3 and 4
    3. Tramp treadles 1 and 3
    4. Tramp treadles 1 and 4
    5. Tramp treadles 2 and 3
    6. Tramp treadles 2 and 4

A draft for "Orange Peeling," a simple coverlet draft, follows:

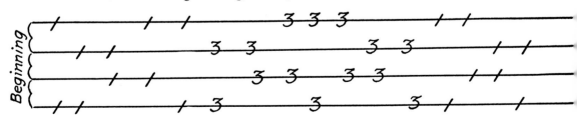

Beginning

This shows that half of the warp threads are carried on harnesses 1 and 2 and the other half, the alternate threads, on harnesses 3 and 4. If, therefore, treadles 1 and 2 are pressed down together, the warp opens in one of the sheds for plain cloth; while by tramping treadles 3 and 4 together the other plain cloth shed opens.

This draft for "Orange Peeling" is drawn in thus: Draw one thread through eye on harness set 1, one thread through harness set 4, one through harness 2, one through harness 4, one through harness 2, one through harness 3, and so on. On reaching the threes in the draft, do not pass three threads through harness set 2 and then three threads through set 4, as would seem to be indicated, but draw in thus: One thread in harness 2, one in harness 4, one in harness 2, one in harness 4, one in harness 2, and one in harness 4. This completes the three threads, and one passes on to the next set of threes, on harnesses 2 and 3. When the end of the draft is reached, go back to the beginning.

The weaving is done in this way, always following the draft: Tramp together treadles 1 and 4, pass the shuttle carrying the colored yarn through the shed. Beat up with sley. Tramp treadles 1 and 2 together, pass through the shed the shuttle carrying the binder, the white cotton thread, and beat up. Tramp treadles 2 and 4, pass through shed the wool yarn, and beat up. Tramp treadles 3 and 4 and pass through shed the cotton binder; and so on, following draft for pattern weaving and opening a plain cloth shed for the binder after each wool thread.

When one comes to the groups of threes, tramp 2 and 4 and pass wool yarn, then open for binder. Repeat the tramping of 2 and 4, with tramping for binder between each, till the wool thread has gone through three times. Then pass on to the next figures on the draft that indicate the tramping of 2 and 4.

On looking at a shed opened for the pattern thread one sees how the pattern-making yarn goes in some places under all the warp threads, in others passes between them as for plain cloth, and in others skips over all threads, so showing pure color.

There are many variations and intricacies in weaving, even by hand and on the old looms, and the history of the development of weaving by hand and by power is a study of absorbing interest and delight. It is well to remember that power weaving is of very recent times, while weaving by hand has ages behind it. The most that can be said for power spinning and weaving has been expressed in these words: "Power weaving has only affected exactness and speed, motive power and ease of changing patterns. It has not increased beauty nor durability. In these it cannot compete with handwork. To many who have made a study of weaving by hand it is plain that no mechanical device can equal in value the human hand in the throwing of the shuttle."

APPENDIX II

DYE PLANTS

LIST of dye plants used in the mountains of North Carolina, identified in 1901 at the Bureau of Plant Industry in Washington, D.C.

Black, brown, gray, bluish, and dull purple.

Name	Part Used	Material Colored
1. *Acer rubrum* L. Red Maple	Bark	Cotton

This bark dyes a fast black, set with copperas. It is also used in combination with witch-hazel or sourwood bark for coloring cotton purple, gray, or black.

Name	Part Used	Material Colored
2. *Juglans cinerea* L. White Walnut or Butternut	Bark, root, leaf, hull	Wool and cotton

Wool—Bark and root used alone or in combination with sumac berries and sourwood leaves to color wool a good and fast black. Bark, root, and hulls used alone or with black-walnut hulls for coloring wool brown. Leaves used for coloring wool brown by immersing in water with wool for three or four weeks.

Cotton—Bark is used for coloring cotton brown. The dye is set with copperas. White walnut is the dye plant most used in the mountains.

Name	Part Used	Material Colored
3. *Juglans nigra* L. Black Walnut	Bark, root, hull	Wool

Used like white walnut for coloring wool black and brown.

Name	Part Used	Material Colored
4. *Platanus occidentalis* L. Sycamore	Bark	Cotton

Used to dye cotton slate color. Set with copperas.

Name	Part Used	Material Colored
5. *Fagus americana* Sweet Synonym, *F. ferruginea* Ail. Beech	Bark	Cotton

Used in combination with witch-hazel to color cotton deep blue or black. Not a fast color, though set with copperas.

(In Britton & Brown, *Flora*, ed. of 1913, it is *Fagus grandifolia* Ehrh.)

Name	*Part Used*	*Material Colored*
6. *Sassafras sassafras* (L) Karst. Sassafras	Root, bark, flower	Wool

The flowers will dye wool bright yellow. The bark colors red-brown, and the root in combination with plum bark dyes also a red-brown.

Name	*Part Used*	*Material Colored*
7. *Quercus prinus* L. Chestnut Oak	Bark	Wool

Dyes wool golden brown. Fast color.

Name	*Part Used*	*Material Colored*
8. *Hamamelis virginiana* L. Witch-hazel, Bead bush	Bark	Cotton

Used only in combination with other barks for dyeing black or gray.

Name	*Part Used*	*Material Colored*
9. *Rhus copallina* L. Black Sumac	Berry	Wool

Used with black and white walnut to color wool black, or with sourwood leaves for the same purpose. The women say that the sumac berries set the dye.

Name	*Part Used*	*Material Colored*
10. *Alnus rugosa* (DuRoi) Koch. Alder	Catkins	Wool and cotton

This dyes wool a yellowish brown, very pretty and a fast color. Dyes cotton brown.

Name	*Part Used*	*Material Colored*
11. *Castanea dentata* (Marsh) Borkh. Chestnut	Bark	Wool

Used with white oak bark to dye dove color.

Name	*Part Used*	*Material Colored*
12. *Prunus americana* Marsh. Wild Plum	Bark	Wool

Used with sassafras root to color red-brown.

Name	*Part Used*	*Material Colored*
13. *Quercus alba* L. White Oak	Bark	Wool

Used with chestnut bark to color dove color. Colors basket splits gray-blue.

Name	*Part Used*	*Material Colored*
14. *Kalmia latifolia* L.	Leaf	Cotton
Mountain Laurel. (Called in North Carolina mountains, Ivy.)		

Colors a purplish gray, not deep but fast. Is set with copperas.

Name	*Part Used*	*Material Colored*
15. *Rhododendron maximum* L.	Leaf	Cotton
Rhododendron. (Called in North Carolina mountains, Laurel.)		

Colors cotton purplish gray; is used like *Kalmia*.

Name	*Part Used*	*Material Colored*
16. *Oxydendrum arboreum* (L) D.C.	Wool and cotton	Leaf
Sourwood		

Used mostly in combination with other dyes as noticed above, for black and purple.

Name	*Part Used*	*Material Colored*
17. *Tsuga canadensis* (L) Carr.	Bark	Wool
Hemlock. (Called in North Carolina mountains, Spruce Pine.)		

Dyes wool a reddish brown. Much depended on as a dye.

Yellow and orange.

(Sassafras flowers, see above, No. 6.)

Name	*Part Used*	*Material Colored*
18. *Symplocos tinctoria* (L) L'Her.	Leaf	Wool
Bay Leaf		

Colors wool a bright yellow. Alum is sometimes used to set the dye but it is fast without this. In the localities where it grows this plant is much used; one of the best known.

Name	*Part Used*	*Material Colored*
19. *Hicoria glabra* (Mill) Britton.	Bark	Wool and cotton
Pig-nut Hickory		

A yellow dye for wool, set with alum. Set with copperas it dyes wool and cotton a good olive green. A much used dye plant.

Name	*Part Used*	*Material Colored*
20. *Andropogon virginicus* L.	Stalk and leaf	Wool
Broom Sedge		

Colors wool yellow. Brighter if set with weak lye. Gathered at any time of year it will color, but the dye is stronger in summer when the plant is green.

Name	*Part Used*	*Material Colored*
21. *Impatiens biflora* Walt. Touch-me-not, or Jewelweed	Stem, leaf, flower	Wool

Dyes wool a dull yellow, if soaked with it in cold water for some weeks.

Name	*Part Used*	*Material Colored*
22. *Coreopsis major* Walt. "Yellow dye flower"	Flower	Wool

A beautiful and fast dye for wool; orange, rather than yellow. Used over a dye of bay leaves it produces a deep reddish orange; very fast color.

Name	*Part Used*	*Material Colored*
23. *Amygdalus persica* L. Peach	Leaf	Wool

This gives a very bright yellow. Some set it with alum. A vivid green is produced by dipping the wool dyed with this into the indigo pot. The leaves are gathered when mature in early autumn.

Name	*Part Used*	*Material Colored*
24. *Quercus velutina* Lam. Synonym, *Q. coccinea tinctoria* Gray. Black Oak	Bark	Wool and cotton

Used as is hickory bark (No. 19) to color yellow and olive green; a better dye than hickory and much esteemed.

Name	*Part Used*	*Material Colored*
25. *Malus coronaria* (L) Mill. Synonym, *Pyrus coronaria.* Crab	Bark	Wool (?)

Said to dye bright yellow. Never tried by us.

Name	*Part Used*	*Material Colored*
26. *Helenium autumnale* L. Sneezeweed, Snuff weed	Flower	Wool

Dyes yellow but must be set with alum. Not even then dependable.

Name	*Part Used*	*Material Colored*
27. *Galium triflorum* Michx. Wild Madder	Whole plant	Wool and cotton

Not strong enough to color red a sufficiently deep color, but when "store madder" was hard to get it was sometimes used as a substitute in the blue pot. (Possibly another species, *Galium tinctorium*, was so used also.)

The two plants below were identified by F. L. Goodrich.

Name	Part Used	Material Colored
28. *Sanguinaria canadensis* L. Bloodroot	Root	Basket splits

A bright orange.

Name	Part Used	Material Colored
29. *Hydrastis canadensis* L. Yellowroot, Goldenseal	Root	Basket splits

Yellow.

INDEX